THE LAKELAND SUMMITS

a survey of the fells of the
Lake District National Park

Timothy Synge

Published by Sigma Leisure - an imprint of
Sigma Press, 1 South Oak Lane, Wilmslow, Cheshire SK9 6AR, England

British Library Cataloguing in Publication Data
A CIP record for this book is available from the British Library

ISBN: 1-85058-446-X

Cover design : The Agency, Wilmslow
Cover photograph : Helm Crag (T.P. Synge)
Printed by: J W Arrowsmith Ltd

Publisher's note : The use of the term 'Wainwright' and the identification of fells included in A.Wainwright's 'Pictorial Guides to the Lakeland Fells' are for ease of reference only. There is no other connection between this book and those of A.Wainwright which are published by Michael Joseph Ltd and in which they hold the copyright.

Disclaimer : The information in this book is given in good faith and is believed to be correct at the time of publication. No responsibility is accepted by either the author or publisher for errors or omissions, or for any loss or injury howsoever caused. You must judge your own fitness, competence and experience.

CONTENTS

INTRODUCTION

This book contains a survey of all the summits lying within the boundary of the Lake District National Park. The survey identifies a total of 646 summits and tabulates every significant summit over 300 metres in height. It also indicates which summits are among the 214 fells included in A. Wainwright's seven Pictorial Guides to the Lakeland Fells, as these books are so widely used. It classifies each summit either as a separate fell or as a subsidiary top, depending upon the amount of re-ascent required to reach the summit.

Area covered

The Lake District National Park covers an area of some 880 square miles. It has, for the purposes of this survey, been divided into regions, whose external boundaries are defined by the outer edges of the National Park itself. Each of these regions is further subdivided, as far as possible into natural groups of fells. Further explanation is provided in the notes to the tables.

Wainwright

It is widely acknowledged that Wainwright's Pictorial Guides to the Lakeland Fells are the finest walking guides to the Lake District. It was realised at an early stage in the preparation of this survey that, because of its comprehensive coverage of the Lake District, the survey would probably include all of the Fells described in the Pictorial Guides and this has subsequently proved to be the case.

Although many would argue that Wainwright selected all the important mountains for inclusion in his guides, it is apparent that a number of other writers of guidebooks (and compilers of lists) have taken exception to some of the great man's choices. Even AW himself acknowledges, when writing about Mungrisdale Common, that 'there is little on these extensive grass slopes to provide even a passing interest for an ordinary walker, and nothing at all to encourage a visit' and that 'precious holiday hours should not be wasted here'. This lack of attraction, when coupled with the almost complete lack of ascent required when approaching the summit from the direction of Blencathra, means that at least one 'Wainwright' remains practically without mention in any other guidebook. However, many people have 'climbed' Mungrisdale Common, and many more will do so. Why? Simply because it is included in the Pictorial Guides.

Walkers who set out to 'do the Wainwrights', self-avowed peakbaggers, might wonder why AW included Mungrisdale Common in his study, yet did not allocate separate chapters to, for example, Broad Crag ('a worthy mountain in itself') and Ill Crag ('a graceful peak when viewed from Upper Eskdale, which it dominates'). Other writers, for example, Terry Marsh and John and Anne Nuttall, have granted separate mountain status to these second and third of the Scafell Pikes. However, many people will never climb these two summits, simply because they are not among the 214 'Wainwrights'.

This survey recognises that the Pictorial Guides are a primary point of reference for many walkers and it has therefore been decided that the 'Wainwrights' should be separately identified in the survey data.

Height

It is usual to regard a Lake District summit of over 2000 feet as a 'mountain'. This may be a tacit acknowledgement that the application of Munro's criteria (3000 feet) would only produce four English mountains; whatever the reason, it certainly permits identification of many of Lakeland's finest summits and peaks as mountains.

Whatever the merits and drawbacks of metrication, one inevitable consequence has been the major revision in the 1970s and 1980s of the maps published by the Ordnance Survey. Heights are all given in metres and the contours are drawn at metric intervals. 2000 feet is about the same as 610 metres. As metric measurements are unlikely to be superseded, it seems logical to adjust this benchmark of 2000 feet to 600 metres. Those who consider that, for example, Illgill Head and White Maiden are not deserving of the nomenclature mountain may of course rule a line across the relevant page of this survey at 610 metres instead.

As the Lake District continues to grow in popularity, not only among walkers but also among writers, many people are turning their attention to the lower fells. The adoption of 2000 feet as a minimum altitude is increasingly exclusive. Turning again to AW, it is interesting to note that the 2000 feet mark is exceeded by 127 of 'his' summits, the 600 metre (1969 feet) mark by a further 3. In either case, this leaves nearly 100 'Wainwrights' languishing below this height. Taking this survey as a whole, a total of 244 summits achieve the 600 metre mark and the remaining 402 do not.

All of these remaining fells, with the sole exception of Castle Crag (for which, partly to demonstrate the ultimately subjective nature of such a survey, an exception has been made), are over 300 metres in height. A clear distinction is made in the survey between summits over 600 metres in height and those below 600 metres in height.

Re-ascent

The preceding notes suggest that it would be churlish to treat all of the fells as being of equal merit. Many attempts have been made to define what constitutes a separate summit with 'independent' status. Some approaches use absolute criteria by which a certain amount of re-ascent is deemed necessary, others apply a combination of factors, for example the minimum re-ascent required and the distance of the fell from neighbouring summits.

This survey makes no apologies for adopting a straightforward approach. If a summit requires a minimum ascent of 30 metres from all sides, it is a separate fell, otherwise it is a subsidiary 'top'. The survey is designed to identify all separate fells over 300 metres in height; the criteria for inclusion of subsidiary tops are of necessity somewhat subjective, as it would, in theory at least, be possible to identify an almost infinite number of such tops, particularly in the sub-600 metre category.

A note of caution for peakbaggers

Readers who may be planning to visit all of the summits in this survey should, to avoid disappointment, note one or two points. Firstly, 'normal' fellwalkers will find a small number of summits rather inaccessible. AW admitted that he had not succeeded in surmounting the highest point of Helm Crag, but an even greater challenge is presented by Pillar Rock. While Pillar Rock is fair game for climbers or even for experienced scramblers who know the route, for ordinary mortals it probably takes on something of the stature of the Inaccessible Pinnacle on Skye, the end of many a Munroist's dreams.

The second obstacle to peakbaggers is the distribution of ownership of land in the Lake District. Even one of the 'Wainwrights', The Nab, is not open to the uninvited walker, and a number of summits on the fringes of the National Park are not on open land. Readers should note that inclusion of such summits in the checklist is not intended to be an inducement to trespass.

6

Feedback

As noted earlier, there is, in spite of the criteria used to define each category, some degree of subjectivity in the selection of summits. If you have any comments on the summits included in or omitted from this survey, I would be interested to hear your views, which could be reflected in future editions of the survey; for example, you might think that the subsidiary tops of Skiddaw merit inclusion or that the 'minor' Crinkle Crags deserve a listing. Letters should be addressed to me via the publisher.

Acknowledgements

Thanks are due to my parents, who provided the £30 (a then not inconsiderable sum) required for my first trip to the Lake District. Ben Sykes introduced me to many areas of the Lakes and was also the first to show me the magic of Wainwright's Pictorial Guides. I must also thank my wife for her unfailing support (not least for prompting us to live without television for over a year, thereby unwittingly giving early impetus to this project) and for putting up with my immersion in this book over many months. And last but not least Katie, who has yet to notch up her first summit and to whom this book is dedicated.

NOTES TO THE TABLES

I. THE SUMMITS BY REGION

The whole of the Lake District National Park has been divided into 47 sections. Each section contains, as far as possible, a natural group of fells which might be the subject of a day's walking or exploration. This has been achieved largely by the use of natural boundaries to divide the District into smaller areas, for example the lakes themselves, rivers and streams. The main exceptions to this are roads, which often follow valley bottoms, and the boundary of the National Park. To impose order on these sections, they have been grouped into seven regions. These regions correspond approximately to the regions used by Wainwright and others, but have been extended outwards (with the obvious exception of the Central Fells) to the boundaries of the National Park. This approach means that outlying fells are included in the relevant region, rather than treated separately.

Section names

Each section has been given a name. This is usually the name of the principal fell in the section and is for reference purposes only.

Maps

For each of the seven main regions described above, a regional map has been drawn to show how the region has been divided into sections. This is followed by separate maps of each of the sections in that region, drawn to a larger scale. It should be noted that these section maps are not all drawn to the same scale, as there is a marked degree of difference in the areas covered, particularly between some of the outlying areas, where the number of fells may be low, and the central areas, where there is generally a higher density of fells.

The maps are designed as guides to the location of the fells rather than as aids to navigation on the fells. For this reason, topographical detail has been kept to a minimum.

Map symbols

The different categories into which the summits have been grouped have already been described in the introduction. A set of map symbols has been devised to represent each category and, by extension, each possible combination of categories.

Firstly, those summits which are also 'Wainwrights' are denoted by triangles and those which are not are given a circular symbol. Secondly, summits of 600 metres or more in height are given a large symbol and those of less than 600 metres a small symbol. Thirdly, for summits with more than 30 metres of re-ascent, the relevant symbol has been shaded, while the symbols of those without have been left unshaded. The full set of symbols is shown in the key to the maps, which appears after these notes. This set of symbols may sound complicated but is in fact very easy to use. For example, Broad Crag, near Scafell Pike, is over 600 metres high and requires 30 metres of re-ascent but is not included by Wainwright. It is therefore depicted on the relevant map by a large shaded circle. Mungrisdale Common, which is a 'Wainwright' over 600 metres high without the required re-ascent, is depicted by a large unshaded triangle.

Other symbols used on the maps are also explained in the key to the maps.

Names of summits

The names of the summits are those used on the Ordnance Survey 1:25 000 scale Outdoor Leisure maps. Where alternative names are in common use, for example on other maps or in popular guidebooks, these are provided in footnotes and are included in the index. Nameless summits (on the OS 1:25000 series, at least) are described as such in the tables. For the purposes of identification, each one has also been annotated with the name of a suitable neighbouring geographical feature, usually the principal fell to which the nameless summit is subsidiary or a nearby crag.

In these tables of the summits by region, the various categories of summit can be distinguished as follows. The 'Wainwrights' are always in capital letters and other fells are in lower case. Separate fells, those requiring over 30 metres of re-ascent, are aligned to the left of the relevant column, while subsidiary tops are indented slightly. As for the distinction between summits over and below 600 metres in height, it is hoped that this will be clear from a study of the height column.

Heights

Heights are those used in the latest Ordnance Survey 1:25000 maps, as these are the maps most widely used by walkers. This is important, as it means that the heights used in the tables should in the main be those which are familiar and which correspond to the maps used. Where a height is not given on the 1:25 000 maps, then the 1:50000 Landranger series has been used. Where a height is not provided by either of these, reference is made to the highest contour shown on the 1:25000 series. It should be assumed that the heights quoted are taken from the 1:25000 series unless otherwise noted.

Many walkers are more familiar with heights in feet, and proud of it. As AW wrote, 'the figures that stay there permanently are Bowfell 2960, Pillar 2927, Scafell Pike 3210 and so on'. In view of the fact that current maps of the Ordnance Survey do not give such information, it has been decided, with much regret, not to include imperial measurements. Readers wishing to assemble details of heights in feet have a number of options. They can refer to older sets of OS maps, they can refer to a wide range of guidebooks for data on many of the principal fells or (and this option will undoubtedly generate errors and is therefore not recommended, except as a rough guide) multiply metric heights by a constant factor.

Readers should note that, inevitably, any analysis of heights in feet will throw up discrepancies between the sources, which may be extremely difficult to reconcile with one another. Recent surveys have, for example, proved a number of widely accepted heights to be incorrect, and a number of guidebook writers have chosen the third option described above.

Grid references

As noted above, the maps in this survey are designed as aids to location of the summits. Grid references are provided to assist accurate pinpointing of each summit on the relevant Ordnance Survey map.

Ordnance Survey maps

In the tables of the summits by region, reference is made to the relevant OS map, both at 1:25000 scale and 1:50 000 scale. The following maps cover the whole of the Lake District National Park at each scale.

1:25000

Pathfinder 567	(NY 24/34)	Wigton
Pathfinder 575	(NY 03/13)	Cockermouth & Maryport
Pathfinder 576	(NY 23/33)	Caldbeck
Outdoor Leisure 4		The English Lakes - North Western area
Outdoor Leisure 5		The English Lakes - North Eastern area
Outdoor Leisure 6		The English Lakes - South Western area
Outdoor Leisure 7		The English Lakes - South Eastern area
Pathfinder 625	(SD 08/18)	Broughton in Furness
Pathfinder 626	(SD 28/38)	Broughton in Furness & Newby Bridge
Pathfinder 627	(SD 48/58)	Milnthorpe
Pathfinder 636	(SD 37/47)	Grange - over- Sands

1:50000

Landranger 85	Carlisle & The Solway Firth
Landranger 89	West Cumbria
Landranger 90	Penrith, Keswick & Ambleside area
Landranger 96	Barrow-in-Furness & South Lakeland area
Landranger 97	Kendal to Morecambe

Order of altitude

The data in the three columns headed 'order of altitude' in the tables of the summits by region has been extracted from the second main section of this survey, the summits in order of altitude. Its inclusion here provides additional guidance to the reader who wishes to ascertain the category or categories to which a summit belongs.

2. THE SUMMITS IN ORDER OF ALTITUDE

In this section of the survey, all 646 summits are listed in order of altitude. In the main, where two or more summits share the same height, they are listed in alphabetical order. Where a contour line has been used to provide a height, it is assumed that this represents a minimum. The effect of this assumption is best explained by means of an example. Little Lingy Hill (600c) is listed above Black Combe (600), but below Seathwaite Fell (601). This approach leads in some cases to summits for which spot heights are not given being 'demoted' by a few places in the table, but is consistent with the treatment of heights as explained earlier.

Summit names given here are the same as those given in the tables of the summits by region.

The final column in this table includes a full reference which enables the reader to locate the summit in the previous tables. This consists firstly of the region reference and secondly of the summit reference as used in that region. For example, in table 5F, summit number 8 is Blencathra, so the reference in this table is given as 5F-8.

3. CHECKLIST

A checklist is provided for those readers who wish to keep a record of the summits which they have visited. This is set out in alphabetical order. Nameless summits have been included under the names appended to them for the purposes of this survey. The height and grid reference of each summit is repeated here and this should help avoid any confusion between summits with the same name. A box is provided for those who wish to record each ascent, together with spaces for the date of (first) ascent and additional notes such as details of the weather, photographs, companions (and this is not intended as an affront to solitary walkers) or any other observations as appropriate.

Whether the reader is interested in visiting every summit in this survey, or whether he or she prefers to focus on one of the subsets, the checklist is extremely easy to use. The symbols used on the maps to represent each type of summit are also included in the checklist, so that it is possible at a glance to pick out, for example, all the fells over 600 metres high just by focusing on the large symbols.

4. INDEX

The survey is rounded off with a full index. This includes alternative names (as included in the footnotes to the tables of the summits by region).

The index indicates where in the tables of the summits by region each summit may be found. If the reader wishes to locate a fell in the table of the summits in order of altitude, reference should first be made to the table of the summits by region to ascertain the height of the fell, which can then be traced by looking at the relevant part of the former table.

KEY TO THE MAPS

+++++++++++++++++++++++++++	Boundary of the Lake District National Park
═══════════════	Road
========================	Track
- - - - - - - - - - - - - - - - -	Path
∼∼∼∼∼∼∼∼	River or stream. Lake or tarn

The summits

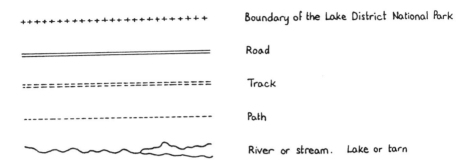

	Over 600 m	Separate fell	'Wainwright'	Symbol
	✓	✓	✓	▲
	✓	✓	✗	●
	✓	✗	✓	△
	✓	✗	✗	○
	✗	✓	✓	▲
	✗	✓	✗	●
	✗	✗	✓	△
	✗	✗	✗	○

These symbols are repeated at the end of the book for ease of reference.

c (following a height)	Highest contour line on 1:25000 map
x (following a height)	Height taken from 1:50000 map

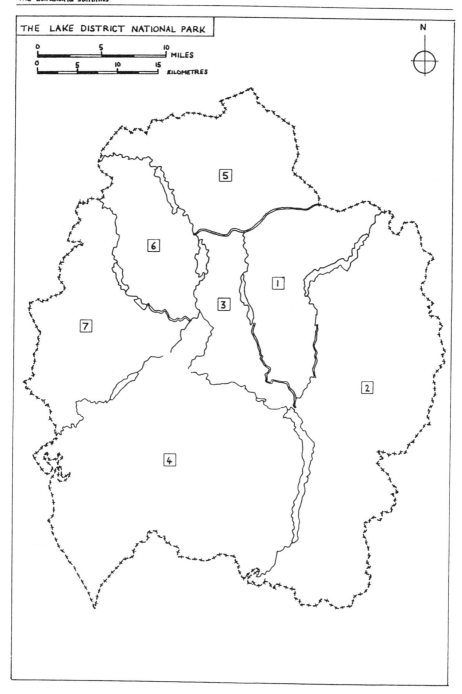

THE LAKE DISTRICT NATIONAL PARK

THE LAKE DISTRICT NATIONAL PARK

1	THE EASTERN FELLS
2	THE FAR EASTERN FELLS
3	THE CENTRAL FELLS
4	THE SOUTHERN FELLS
5	THE NORTHERN FELLS
6	THE NORTH WESTERN FELLS
7	THE WESTERN FELLS

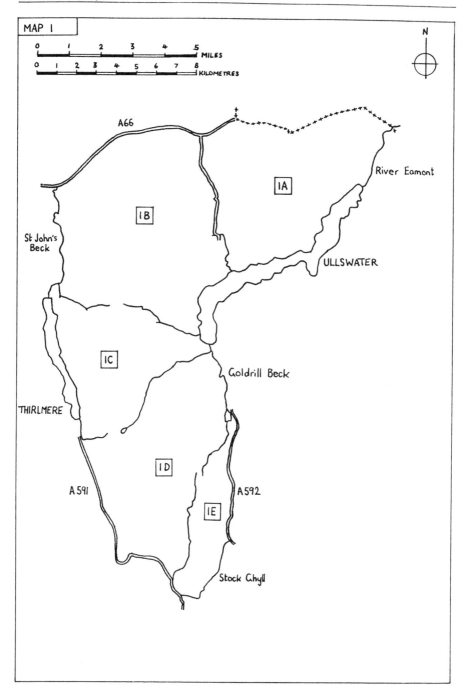

MAP 1

MILES

KILOMETRES

N

A66

River Eamont

1A

1B

St John's Beck

ULLSWATER

1C

Goldrill Beck

THIRLMERE

1D

A 591

A 592

1E

Stock Ghyll

TABLE I
THE EASTERN FELLS

IA	MATTERDALE
IB	THE DODDS
IC	HELVELLYN
ID	FAIRFIELD
IE	RED SCREES

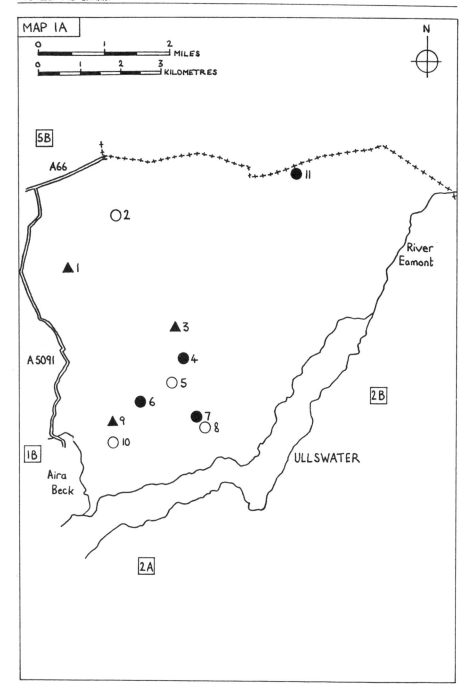

MAP 1A

0 1 2 MILES
0 1 2 3 KILOMETRES

N

5B

A66

2B

River Eamont

○2

▲1

A5091

▲3

●4

○5

●6

▲9

○10

●7
○8

1B

Aira
Beck

2B

●11

ULLSWATER

2A

TABLE IA
THE EASTERN FELLS - MATTERDALE

| No. | Name | Grid ref. | Ht. | No. in order of altitude | | | OS map no. | |
				Fell	Top	AW	1:25000	1:50000
I	GREAT MELL FELL	397254	537	141	314	155	OL-NE	90
2	Brownhow Hill	408266	305	-	634	-	OL-NE	90
3	LITTLE MELL FELL	423240	505	161	365	173	OL-NE	90
4	Nameless summit (Little Mell Fell - S.Top)	425233	424	198	471	-	OL-NE	90
5	Little Meldrum	422228	404	-	507	-	OL-NE	90
6	Great Meldrum	415223	437	193	454	-	OL-NE	90
7	Hagg Wood	428220	342	228	576	-	OL-NE	90
8	Birk Crag	430218	319x	-	612	-	OL-NE	90
9	GOWBARROW FELL	408218	481	175	404	181	OL-NE	90
10	Gowbarrow Park¹	408214	464	-	422	-	OL-NE	90
11	Dacre Bank	451276	302	254	640	-	OL-NE	90

1. Green Hill

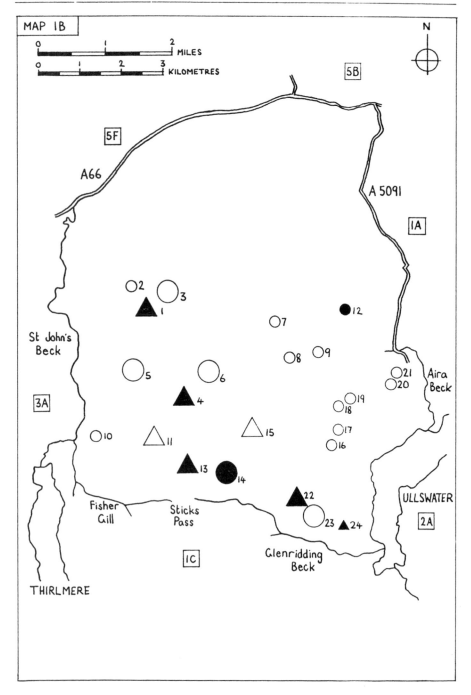

TABLE 1B
THE EASTERN FELLS - THE DODDS

| No. | Name | Grid ref. | Ht. | No. in order of altitude | | | OS map no. | |
				Fell	Top	AW	1:25000	1:50000
1	CLOUGH HEAD	334225	726	71	116	74	OL-NE	90
2	Threlkeld Knotts	330230	514	–	348	–	OL-NE	90
3	White Pike	339229	620c	–	221	–	OL-NE	90
4	GREAT DODD	342206	857	20	27	19	OL-NE	90
5	Calfhow Pike	331211	660c	–	170	–	OL-NE	90
6	Randerside	349211	720c	–	120	–	OL-NE	90
7	Nameless summit (Matterdale Common)	364222	541	–	307	–	OL-NE	90
8	High Brow	368214	575	–	261	–	OL-NE	90
9	Low How	374215	497	–	379	–	OL-NE	90
10	Castle Rock	322197	339	–	580	–	OL-NE	90
11	WATSON'S DODD	336196	789	–	60	41	OL-NE	90
12	Cockley Moor	381225	455	184	431	–	OL-NE	90
13	STYBARROW DODD	343189	843	22	31	21	OL-NE	90
14	Green Side [1]	353188	795	40	56	–	OL-NE	90
15	HART SIDE	359198	756	–	89	61	OL-NE	90
16	Brown Hills	378194	550	–	294	–	OL-NE	90
17	Swineside Knott	379197	553	–	286	–	OL-NE	90
18	Watermillock Common	379203	540c	–	311	–	OL-NE	90
19	Common Fell	382205	550	–	295	–	OL-NE	90
20	Round How	392208	387	–	535	–	OL-NE	90
21	Bracken How	393211	370c	–	548	–	OL-NE	90
22	SHEFFIELD PIKE	369182	675	89	157	99	OL-NE	90
23	Heron Pike	373178	610c	–	229	–	OL-NE	90
24	GLENRIDDING DODD	381175	442	191	446	191	OL-NE	90

1. White Stones

21

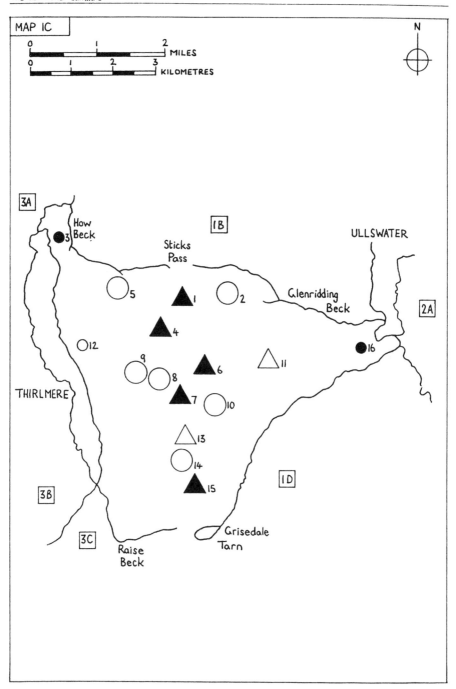

MAP IC

0   1   2 MILES
0   1   2   3 KILOMETRES

N

3A

How Beck
●3

1B

Sticks Pass

ULLSWATER

○5
▲1
○2

Glenridding Beck

2A

▲4

○12

○9
○8
▲6
△11
●16

THIRLMERE

▲7
○10

△13

○14

▲15

1D

3B

3C

Grisedale Tarn

Raise Beck

TABLE IC
THE EASTERN FELLS - HELVELLYN

| No. | Name | Grid ref. | Ht. | No. in order of altitude | | | OS map no. | |
				Fell	Top	AW	1:25000	1:50000
1	RAISE	343174	883	13	16	12	OL-NE	90
2	Stang	354175	670c	-	163	-	OL-NE	90
3	Great How	313187	330c	237	597	-	OL-NE	90
4	WHITE SIDE [1]	338167	863	17	21	16	OL-NE	90
5	Brown Crag	328177	610	-	232	-	OL-NE	90
6	CATSTYE CAM	348158	890	11	14	10	OL-NE	90
7	HELVELLYN	342151	950	3	4	3	OL-NE	90
8	Lower Man	337155	925	-	8	-	OL-NE	90
9	Browncove Crags	332157	859x	-	24	-	OL-NE	90
10	High Spying How [2]	351149	860c	-	23	-	OL-NE	90
11	BIRKHOUSE MOOR	364160	718	-	123	78	OL-NE	90
12	The Swirls	319163	330c	-	599	-	OL-NE	90
13	NETHERMOST PIKE	344142	891	-	13	9	OL-NE	90
14	High Crag	343137	880c	-	17	-	OL-NE	90
15	DOLLYWAGGON PIKE	346131	858	19	26	18	OL-NE	90
16	Keldas	385163	311	249	624	-	OL-NE	90

1. Whiteside Bank
2. Striding Edge

23

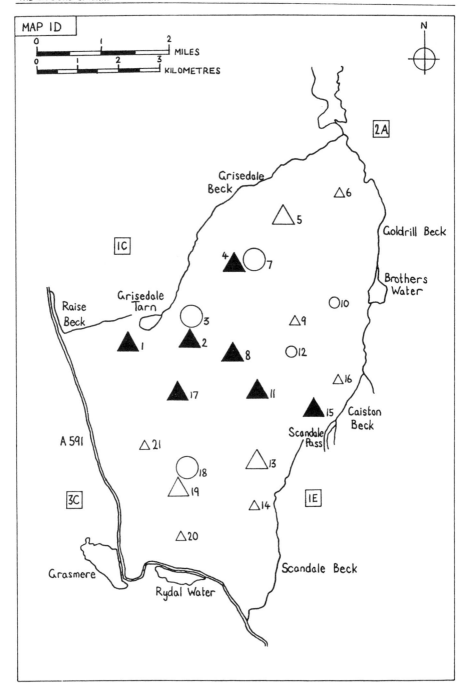

TABLE 1D
THE EASTERN FELLS - FAIRFIELD

No.	Name	Grid ref	Ht.	No. in order of altitude			OS map no.	
				Fell	Top	AW	1:25000	1:50000
1	SEAT SANDAL	344115	736	67	106	69	OL-NE	90
2	FAIRFIELD	359118	873	14	18	13	OL-NE	90
3	Cofa Pike	359121	820c	-	40	-	OL-NE	90
4	ST SUNDAY CRAG	369134	841	24	33	23	OL-NE	90
5	BIRKS	380144	622	-	216	124	OL-NE	90
6	ARNISON CRAG	394150	433	-	457	194	OL-NE	90
7	Gavel Pike	373134	784	-	63	-	OL-NE	90
8	HART CRAG	368113	822	30	39	27	OL-NE	90
9	HARTSOP ABOVE HOW [1]	384120	580c	-	258	137	OL-NE	90
10	Gale Crag	392124	512	-	350	-	OL-NE	90
11	DOVE CRAG	374105	792	41	57	38	OL-NE	90
12	Stangs	382113	470c	-	415	-	OL-NE	90
13	HIGH PIKE [2]	374088	656	-	178	109	OL-SE	90
14	LOW PIKE	374078	508	-	362	172	OL-SE	90
15	LITTLE HART CRAG	387100	637	106	199	120	OL-NE	90
16	HIGH HARTSOP DODD	394108	519	-	342	165	OL-NE	90
17	GREAT RIGG	356104	766	54	80	54	OL-NE	90
18	Rydal Fell	357087	621	-	217	-	OL-SE	90
19	HERON PIKE	356083	612	-	227	127	OL-SE	90
20	NAB SCAR	355072	440c	-	450	193	OL-SE	90
21	STONE ARTHUR	348092	500c	-	373	175	OL-SE	90

1. Gill Crag
2. Scandale Fell

25

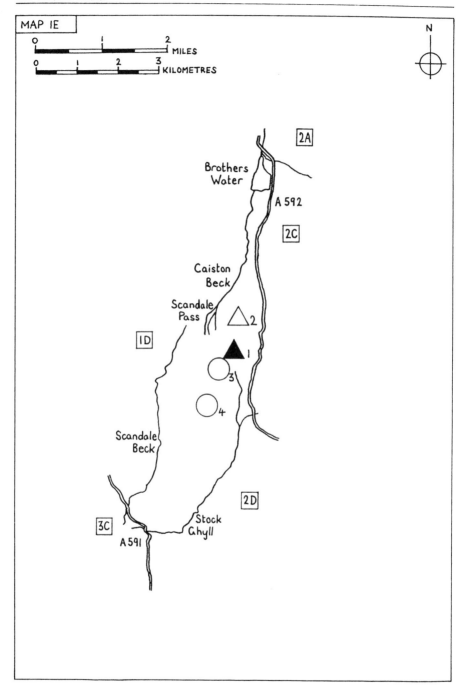

MAP IE

0   1   2
MILES

0   1   2   3
KILOMETRES

N

2A

Brothers
Water

A 592

2C

Caiston
Beck

Scandale
Pass

1D

2

1

3

4

Scandale
Beck

2D

Stock
Ghyll

3C

A 591

TABLE IE
THE EASTERN FELLS - RED SCREES

| No. | Name | Grid ref. | Ht. | No. in order of altitude | | | OS map no. | |
				Fell	Top	AW	1:25000	1:50000
1	RED SCREES	396088	776	50	72	49	OL-SE	90
2	MIDDLE DODD	397096	654	-	181	111	OL-SE	90
3	Raven Crag	394084	750c	-	95	-	OL-SE	90
4	Snarker Pike	390075	644	-	190	-	OL-SE	90

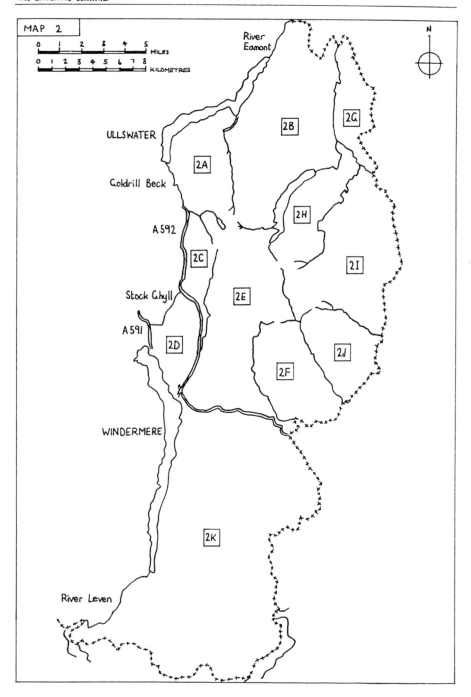

MAP 2

0 1 2 3 4 5 MILES
0 1 2 3 4 5 6 7 8 KILOMETRES

N

River Eamont

ULLSWATER

2B

2G

2A

Goldrill Beck

A592

2H

2C

2I

Stock Ghyll

2E

A591

2D

2J

2F

WINDERMERE

2K

River Leven

TABLE 2
THE FAR EASTERN FELLS

2A	PLACE FELL AND REST DODD
2B	HIGH STREET (NORTH)
2C	CAUDALE MOOR
2D	WANSFELL
2E	KENTMERE
2F	HOLLOW MOOR AND BRUNT KNOTT
2G	KNIPE SCAR
2H	BRANSTREE AND SELSIDE PIKE
2I	GREY CRAG AND THE SHAP FELLS
2J	BANNISDALE
2K	GUMMER'S HOW

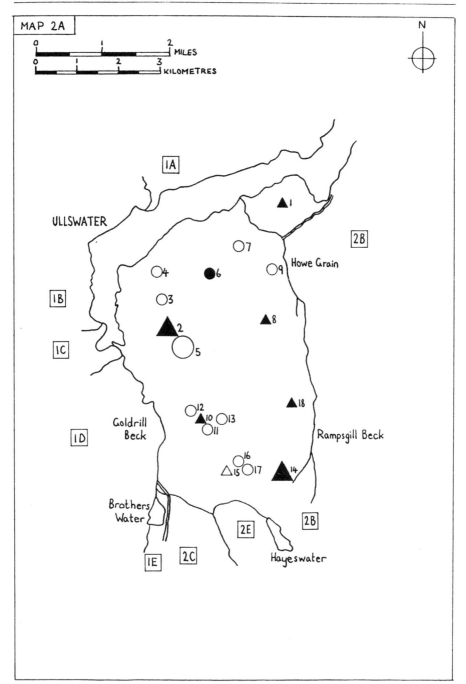

MAP 2A

ULLSWATER

1A

2B

Howe Grain

1B

1C

1D

Goldrill
Beck

Rampsgill Beck

Brothers
Water

2E

2B

1E

2C

Hayeswater

TABLE 2A
THE FAR EASTERN FELLS - PLACE FELL AND REST DODD

No.	Name	Grid ref.	Ht.	No. in order of altitude			OS map no.	
				Fell	Top	AW	1:25000	1:50000
1	HALLIN FELL	433198	388	214	534	203	OL-NE	90
2	PLACE FELL	406170	657	96	177	108	OL-NE	90
3	The Knight	404176	550c	-	293	-	OL-NE	90
4	Birk Fell [1]	403183	510c	-	355	-	OL-NE	90
5	Round How	408166	630c	-	209	-	OL-NE	90
6	High Dodd	415182	501	163	370	-	OL-NE	90
7	Sleet Fell	422188	378	-	541	-	OL-NE	90
8	BEDA HEAD [2]	428170	509	158	358	170	OL-NE	90
9	Winter Crag	430183	330c	-	600	-	OL-NE	90
10	ANGLETARN PIKES	414148	567	128	274	143	OL-NE	90
11	Angletarn Pikes	414147	565	-	275	-	OL-NE	90
12	Stony Rigg	411151	500c	-	374	-	OL-NE	90
13	Heck Crag	418149	550c	-	291	-	OL-NE	90
14	REST DODD	432137	696	85	144	92	OL-NE	90
15	BROCK CRAGS	417137	561	-	278	144	OL-NE	90
16	Buck Crag	422139	570c	-	269	·	OL-NE	90
17	Satura Crag	424137	560c	-	281	-	OL-NE	90
18	THE NAB	434152	576	123	260	139	OL-NE	90

1. Bleaberry Knott
2. BEDA FELL

31

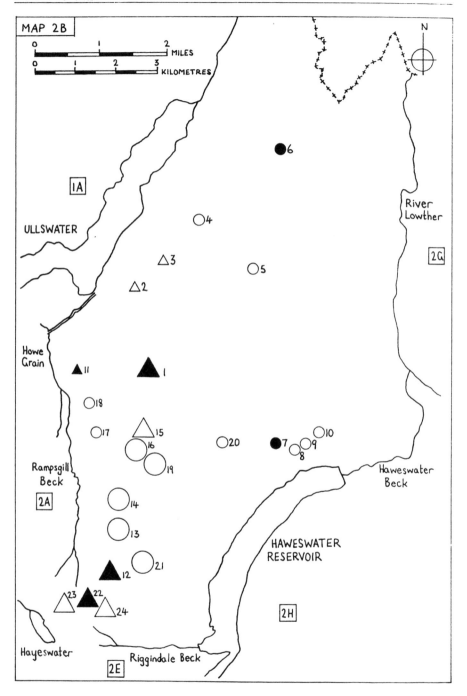

MAP 2B

0   1   2   MILES

0   1   2   3   KILOMETRES

1A

ULLSWATER

Howe
Grain

Rampsgill
Beck

2A

N

River
Lowther

2G

Haweswater
Beck

HAWESWATER
RESERVOIR

2H

Hayeswater

Riggindale Beck

2E

TABLE 2B
THE FAR EASTERN FELLS - HIGH STREET (NORTH)

No.	Name	Grid ref.	Ht.	No. in order of altitude			OS map no.	
				Fell	Top	AW	1:25000	1:50000
1	LOADPOT HILL	457181	671	91	161	102	OL-NE	90
2	BONSCALE PIKE	453200	524x	-	332	161	OL-NE	90
3	ARTHUR'S PIKE	461207	532x	-	317	157	OL-NE	90
4	White Knott	469215	420c	-	480	-	OL-NE	90
5	Knotts	482204	406x	-	503	-	OL-NE	90
6	Heughscar Hill	488231	375x	216	543	-	OL-NE	90
7	Nameless summit (Bampton Common)	487165	489	168	390	-	OL-NE	90
8	Four Stones Hill	492163	415	-	483	-	OL-NE	90
9	Little Birkhouse Hill	494165	400c	-	514	-	OL-NE	90
10	Pinnacle Howe	497167	380c	-	538	-	OL-NE	90
11	STEEL KNOTTS [1]	440181	432	194	460	195	OL-NE	90
12	HIGH RAISE	448135	802	34	48	31	OL-NE	90
13	Raven Howe	450145	710c	-	128	-	OL-NE	90
14	Red Crag	450152	711	-	127	-	OL-NE	90
15	WETHER HILL	456167	670c	-	164	103	OL-NE	90
16	Wether Hill	454163	670c	-	165	-	OL-NE	90
17	Gowk Hill	445167	470c	-	414	-	OL-NE	90
18	Brownthwaite Crag	443174	444	-	444	-	OL-NE	90
19	High Kop	458160	660c	-	173	-	OL-NE	90
20	Low Kop	474165	572	-	266	-	OL-NE	90
21	Low Raise	456138	754	-	92	-	OL-NE	90
22	RAMPSGILL HEAD	443128	792	42	58	39	OL-NE	90
23	THE KNOTT	437127	739	-	103	66	OL-NE	90
24	KIDSTY PIKE	447126	780c	-	68	46	OL-NE	90

1. Pikeawassa

33

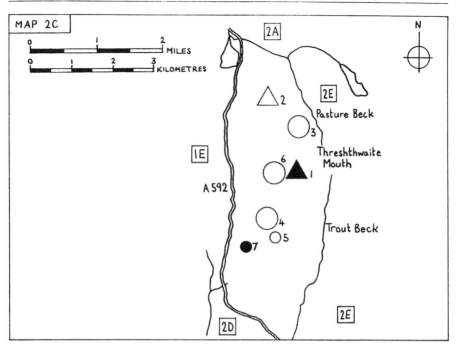

MAP 2C

0   1   2 MILES

0   1   2   3 KILOMETRES

2A

2E

Pasture Beck

Threshthwaite Mouth

1E

A 592

Trout Beck

2E

2D

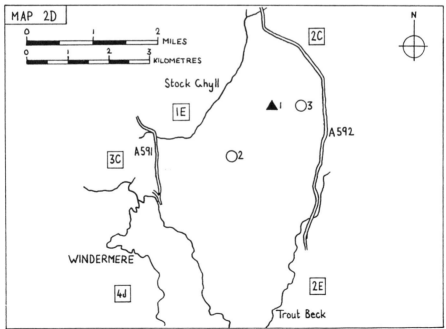

MAP 2D

0   1   2 MILES

0   1   2   3 KILOMETRES

Stock Ghyll

2C

1E

A 592

3C   A591

WINDERMERE

4J

2E

Trout Beck

TABLE 2C
THE FAR EASTERN FELLS - CAUDALE MOOR

| No. | Name | Grid ref. | Ht. | No. in order of altitude | | | OS map no. | |
				Fell	Top	AW	1:25000	1:50000
1	STONY COVE PIKE [1]	418100	763	55	81	55	OL-NE	90
2	HARTSOP DODD	411118	618	-	222	125	OL-NE	90
3	Raven Crag	419111	610c	-	230	-	OL-NE	90
4	Pike How	411090	620c	-	220	-	OL-SE	90
5	Hart Crag	413086	590c	-	249	-	OL-SE	90
6	Caudale Moor	413101	750c	-	94	-	OL-NE	90
7	St Raven's Edge	406084	593	118	247	-	OL-SE	90

TABLE 2D
THE FAR EASTERN FELLS - WANSFELL

| No. | Name | Grid ref. | Ht. | No. in order of altitude | | | OS map no. | |
				Fell	Top	AW	1:25000	1:50000
1	BAYSTONES [2]	404053	487	171	394	178	OL-SE	90
2	Wansfell Pike	394042	484	-	397	-	OL-SE	90
3	Dod Hill	411053	451	-	435	-	OL-SE	90

1. CAUDALE MOOR or John Bell's Banner
2. WANSFELL

35

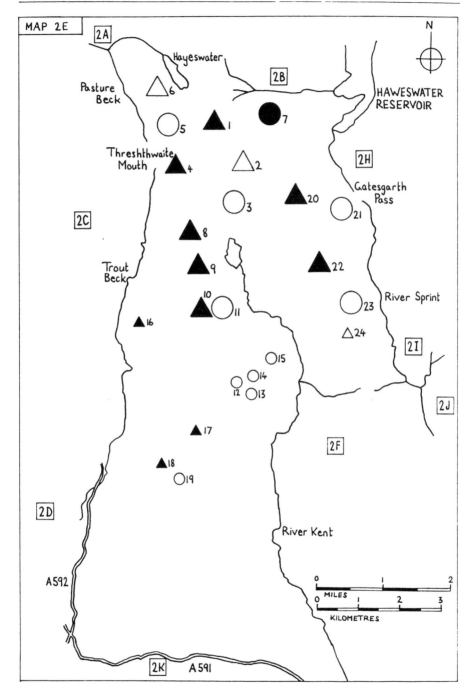

TABLE 2E
THE FAR EASTERN FELLS - KENTMERE

| No. | Name | Grid ref | Ht. | No.in order of altitude | | | OS map no. | |
				Fell	Top	AW	1:25000	1:50000
1	HIGH STREET	441111	828	28	37	25	OL-NE	90
2	MARDALE ILL BELL	448101	760c	-	86	59	OL-NE	90
3	Lingmell End	446092	660c	-	174	-	OL-SE	90
4	THORNTHWAITE CRAG	432101	784	46	64	43	OL-NE	90
5	Nameless summit (Thornthwaite Crag -N.Ridge)	430110	710	-	130	-	OL-NE	90
6	GRAY CRAG	428117	699	-	141	90	OL-NE	90
7	Rough Crag	454112	628	110	210	-	OL-NE	90
8	FROSWICK	435085	720	74	121	77	OL-SE	90
9	ILL BELL	437077	757	58	88	60	OL-SE	90
10	YOKE	438067	706	81	133	85	OL-SE	90
11	Rainsborrow Crag	441068	640c	-	194	-	OL-SE	90
12	Castle Crag	446052	490	-	389	-	OL-SE	90
13	Piked Howes	450048	407	-	502	-	OL-SE	90
14	Rowantree Knotts	450052	420c	-	479	-	OL-SE	90
15	Scale Knotts	455056	360c	-	561	-	OL-SE	90
16	THE TONGUE [1]	422064	364	221	556	207	OL-SE	90
17	SALLOWS	437040	516	156	345	166	OL-SE	90
18	SOUR HOWES	428032	483	174	402	180	OL-SE	90
19	Capple Howe	432029	445	-	443	-	OL-SE	90
20	HARTER FELL	460093	778	49	71	48	OL-SE	90
21	Adam Seat	471091	666	-	166	-	OL-SE	90
22	KENTMERE PIKE	466078	730	69	114	72	OL-SE	90
23	Goat Scar	473069	626	-	215	-	OL-SE	90
24	SHIPMAN KNOTTS	473063	587	-	254	133	OL-SE	90

1. TROUTBECK TONGUE

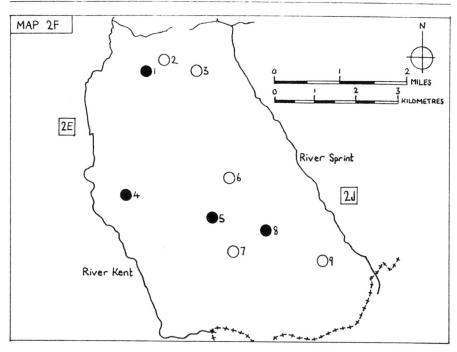

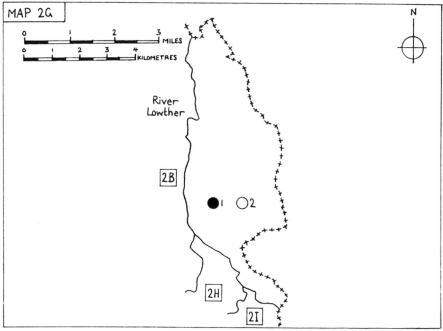

TABLE 2F
THE FAR EASTERN FELLS - HOLLOW MOOR AND BRUNT KNOTT

No.	Name	Grid ref.	Ht.	No. in order of altitude			OS map no.	
				Fell	Top	AW	1:25000	1:50000
1	Hollow Moor [1]	469040	426	197	468	-	OL-SE	90
2	Nameless summit (Hollow Moor-E.Top)	473042	410c	-	492	-	OL-SE	90
3	Cocklaw Fell	481038	365	-	554	-	OL-SE	90
4	Millrigg Knott	464011	300	256	645	-	OL-SE	90
5	Brunt Knott	484006	427	195	465	-	OL-SE	90
6	Sleddale Forest	488016	429	-	463	-	OL-SE	90
7	Nameless summit (Brunt Knott-S.Top)	489998	395	-	521	-	OL-SE	97
8	Nameless summit (Potter Fell)	497003	390	212	532	-	OL-SE	90
9	Ulgroves	511996	332x	-	594	-	OL-SE	97

TABLE 2G
THE FAR EASTERN FELLS - KNIPE SCAR

No.	Name	Grid ref.	Ht.	No. in order of altitude			OS map no.	
				Fell	Top	AW	1:25000	1:50000
1	Knipe Scar	527191	342	229	577	-	OL-NE	90
2	In Scar	536191	342	-	578	-	OL-NE	90

1. Green Quarter Fell

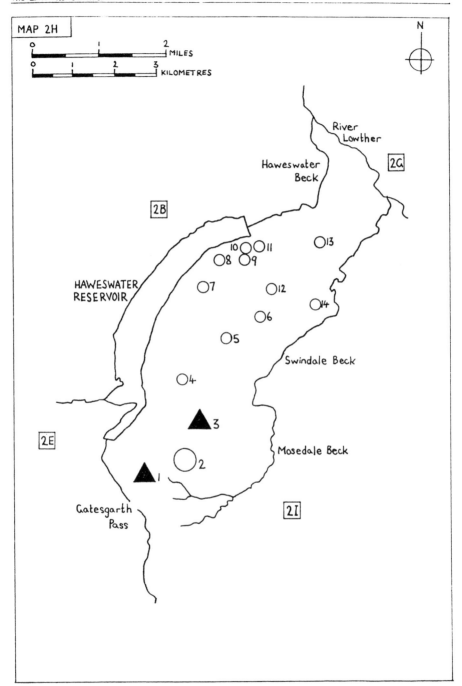

MAP 2H

MILES

KILOMETRES

N

River Lowther

Haweswater Beck

2G

2B

HAWESWATER RESERVOIR

○10 ○11
○8 ○9
○13
○7
○12
○14
○6
○5
Swindale Beck
○4
▲3
Mosedale Beck
○2
▲1

2E

2I

Gatesgarth Pass

TABLE 2H
THE FAR EASTERN FELLS - BRANSTREE AND SELSIDE PIKE

No.	Name	Grid ref.	Ht.	No. in order of altitude			OS map no.	
				Fell	Top	AW	1:25000	1:50000
1	BRANSTREE [1]	478100	713	78	126	81	OL-NE	90
2	Nameless summit (Branstree-E.Top)	488103	673	-	159	-	OL-NE	90
3	SELSIDE PIKE	490112	655	97	180	110	OL-NE	90
4	Rowantreethwaite	487122	529	-	323	-	OL-NE	90
5	Hare Shaw	498131	503	-	366	-	OL-NE	90
6	Powley's Hill	505135	465	-	421	-	OL-NE	90
7	Kit Crag [2]	492143	435	-	455	-	OL-NE	90
8	Wallow Crag	496149	430c	-	462	-	OL-NE	90
9	Low Forest	502150	426	-	470	-	OL-NE	90
10	Hugh's Laithes Pike	502152	410c	-	493	-	OL-NE	90
11	Nameless summit (Naddle Farm Top)	505152	395	-	523	-	OL-NE	90
12	Harper Hills	508143	419	-	481	-	OL-NE	90
13	Scalebarrow Knott	520153	338x	-	582	-	OL-NE	90
14	Swindale Foot Crag	518139	380	-	539	-	OL-NE	90

1. Artlecrag Pike
2. High Forest

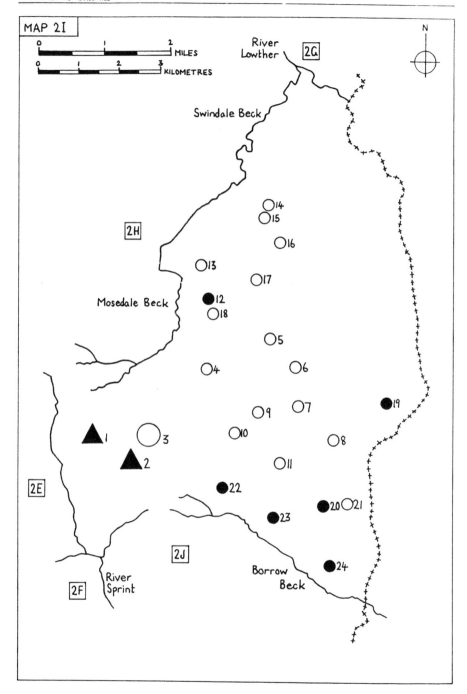

TABLE 2I
THE FAR EASTERN FELLS - GREY CRAG AND THE SHAP FELLS

| No. | Name | Grid ref. | Ht. | No. in order of altitude | | | OS map no. | |
				Fell	Top	AW	1:25000	1:50000
1	TARN CRAG	488078	664	92	168	104	OL-SE	90
2	GREY CRAG '	497072	638	104	196	118	OL-SE	90
3	Harrop Pike	501078	637	-	198	-	OL-SE	90
4	Ulthwaite Rigg	514093	502x	-	368	-	OL-SE	90
5	Tongue Rigg	530100	440c	-	451	-	OL-SE	90
6	Sleddale Pike	535094	500c	-	372	-	OL-SE	90
7	Wasdale Pike	536084	565	-	276	-	OL-SE	90
8	Hazel Bank	545077	427	-	467	-	OL-SE	90
9	Great Saddle Crag	526084	560c	-	280	-	OL-SE	90
10	Great Yarlside	521079	590c	-	248	-	OL-SE	90
11	Little Yarlside	532072	516	-	344	-	OL-SE	90
12	High Wether Howe	515109	531	143	318	-	OL-NE	90
13	Fewling Stones	513118	500c	-	371	-	OL-NE	90
14	Langhowe Pike	530131	405	-	505	-	OL-NE	90
15	Rowantree Crag	529128	400c	-	516	-	OL-NE	90
16	Great Ladstones	532122	440c	-	449	-	OL-NE	90
17	Seat Robert	527114	515	-	347	-	OL-NE	90
18	Scam Matthew	516105	520c	-	341	-	OL-NE	90
19	Long Fell	557085	452	185	433	-	OL-SE	90
20	Whatshaw Common	542061	485	172	396	-	OL-SE	90
21	Nameless summit (Whatshaw Common - E.Top)	548062	484	-	398	-	OL-SE	90
22	Lord's Seat	518066	524	152	333	-	OL-SE	90
23	Robin Hood	530059	493	167	385	-	OL-SE	90
24	High House Bank	543048	495	164	381	-	OL-SE	90

1. Sleddale Fell

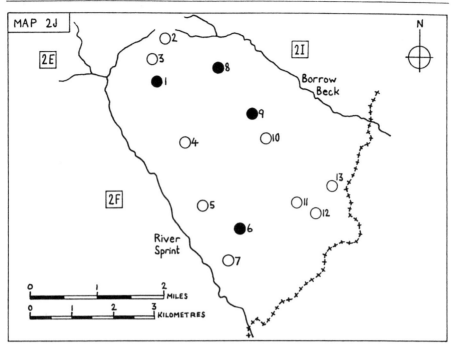

MAP 2J

2E

2I

Borrow
Beck

2F

River
Sprint

0   1   2
|————————|————————| MILES
0   1   2   3
|————|————|————| KILOMETRES

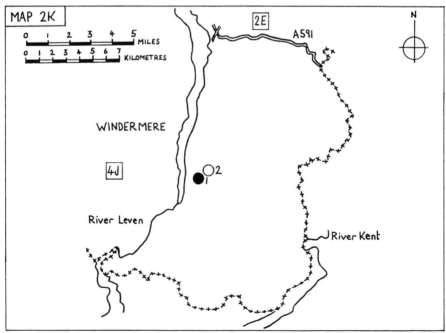

MAP 2K

0   1   2   3   4   5
|—|—|—|—|—|—| MILES
0 1 2 3 4 5 6 7
|—|—|—|—|—|—|—| KILOMETRES

2E

A591

WINDERMERE

4J

River Leven

River Kent

TABLE 2J
THE FAR EASTERN FELLS - BANNISDALE

No.	Name	Grid ref.	Ht.	No. in order of altitude			OS map no.	
				Fell	Top	AW	1:25000	1:50000
1	Swinklebank Crag	501049	553	133	287	-	OL-SE	90
2	Nameless summit (Ancrow Brow-N.Top)	503059	541	-	304	-	OL-SE	90
3	Ancrow Brow	500055	540c	-	308	-	OL-SE	90
4	Capplebarrow	508034	512	-	349	-	OL-SE	90
5	Todd Fell	512021	401	-	511	-	OL-SE	90
6	Whiteside Pike	521015	397	208	519	-	OL-SE	90
7	Murthwaite Knott	518009	300c	-	643	-	OL-SE	90
8	Bannisdale Fell	516052	493	166	384	-	OL-SE	90
9	White Howe	524042	530	144	320	-	OL-SE	90
10	The Forest	528036	528	-	325	-	OL-SE	90
11	Lamb Pasture	534021	367	-	553	-	OL-SE	90
12	Nameless summit (Lamb Pasture-S.E.Top)	539018	332	-	592	-	OL-SE	90
13	Wolf Howe	543024	331	-	596	-	OL-SE	90

TABLE 2K
THE FAR EASTERN FELLS - GUMMER'S HOW

No.	Name	Grid ref.	Ht.	No. in order of altitude			OS map no.	
				Fell	Top	AW	1:25000	1:50000
1	Gummer's How	390885	321	243	607	-	PF626	97
2	Birch Fell	395892	318	-	615	-	PF626	97

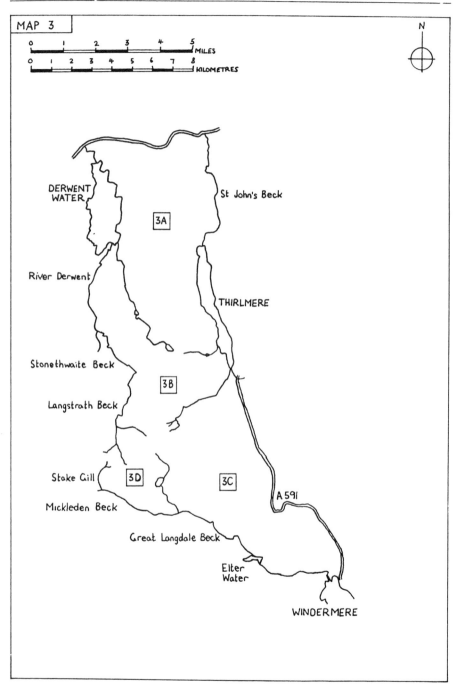

TABLE 3
THE CENTRAL FELLS

3A	BLEABERRY FELL AND HIGH SEAT
3B	ULLSCARF
3C	HIGH RAISE
3D	THE LANGDALES

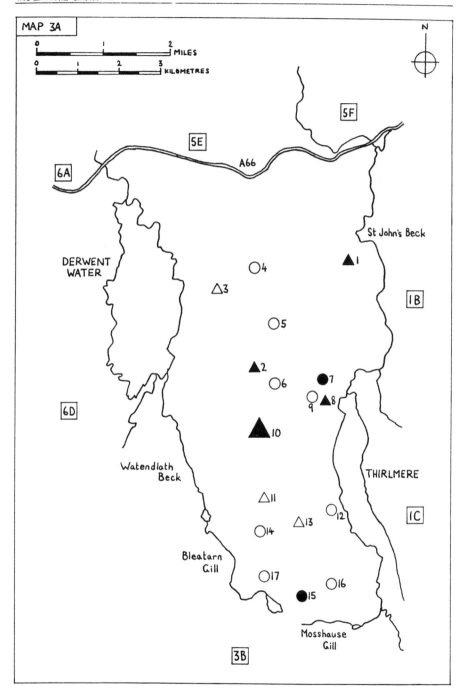

MAP 3A

0   1   2 MILES

0   1   2   3 KILOMETRES

N

5F

5E

A66

6A

St John's Beck

DERWENT
WATER

○4

△3

△1

1B

○5

▲2

○6

●7

○9 ▲8

▲10

6D

Watendlath
Beck

THIRLMERE

△11

△13

○12

1C

○14

Bleatarn
Gill

○17

○16

●15

Mosshause
Gill

3B

TABLE 3A
THE CENTRAL FELLS - BLEABERRY FELL AND HIGH SEAT

No.	Name	Grid ref.	Ht.	Fell	Top	AW	1:25000	1:50000
1	HIGH RIGG	307 215	343	227	574	210	OL-NW	90
2	BLEABERRY FELL	286 196	590	119	251	132	OL-NW	90
3	WALLA CRAG	277 213	379	-	540	204	OL-NW	90
4	Pike	286 218	359x	-	563	-	OL-NW	90
5	Dodd Crag	291 206	460c	-	427	-	OL-NW	90
6	Nameless summit (Bleaberry Fell - S.E. Top)	291 191	570c	-	268	-	OL-NW	90
7	Sippling Crag [1]	302 193	446	190	442	-	OL-NW	90
8	RAVEN CRAG	305 188	461	180	424	186	OL-NW	90
9	Castle Crag	300 188	400c	-	512	-	OL-NW	90
10	HIGH SEAT	287 180	608	115	236	129	OL-NW	90
11	HIGH TOVE	289 165	515	-	346	167	OL-NW	90
12	Fisher Crag	305 163	420c	-	476	-	OL-NW	90
13	ARMBOTH FELL	297 160	479	-	407	182	OL-NW	90
14	Middle Crag	288 158	484x	-	399	-	OL-NW	90
15	Bell Crags	298 143	558	130	282	-	OL-NW	90
16	Brown Rigg	305 146	463	-	423	-	OL-NW	90
17	Long Moss	289 148	510c	-	356	-	OL-NW	90

1. The Benn

49

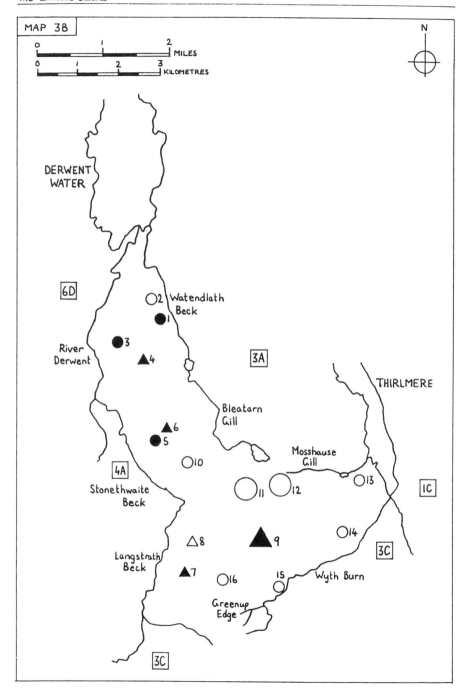

MAP 3B

N

0   1   2 MILES

0   1   2   3 KILOMETRES

DERWENT
WATER

6D

○2 Watendlath
Beck

●1

River
Derwent

●3

▲4

3A

THIRLMERE

Bleatarn
Gill

▲6

●5

Mosshause
Gill

○10

4A

○11 ○12

○13

1C

Stonethwaite
Beck

△8

▲9

○14

3C

Langstrath
Beck

▲7

○16

15○

Wyth Burn

Greenup
Edge

3C

TABLE 3B
THE CENTRAL FELLS - ULLSCARF

| No. | Name | Grid ref. | Ht. | No. in order of altitude | | | OS map no. | |
				Fell	Top	AW	1:25000	1:50000
1	Ether Knott	268172	410c	202	491	-	OL-NW	90
2	Brown Dodd	266177	360c	-	559	-	OL-NW	90
3	King's How	258166	392	210	526	-	OL-NW	90
4	BRUND FELL '	264162	410c	201	490	200	OL-NW	90
5	Knotts	267144	400c	207	513	-	OL-NW	90
6	GREAT CRAG	270147	440c	192	448	192	OL-NW	90
7	SERGEANT'S CRAG	274114	571	126	267	141	OL-NW	90
8	EAGLE CRAG	276121	520c	-	340	164	OL-NW	90
9	ULLSCARF	292122	726	72	117	75	OL-NW	90
10	High Crag	274139	450c	-	437	-	OL-NW	90
11	Low Saddle	288133	656	-	179	-	OL-NW	90
12	Standing Crag	296134	610c	-	231	-	OL-NW	90
13	Birk Crag	315135	357x	-	565	-	OL-NW	90
14	Nab Crags	312125	508	-	363	-	OL-NW	90
15	Middle How	296110	483	-	401	-	OL-NW	90
16	Lining Crag	283112	540c	-	310	-	OL-NW	90

1. GRANGE FELL

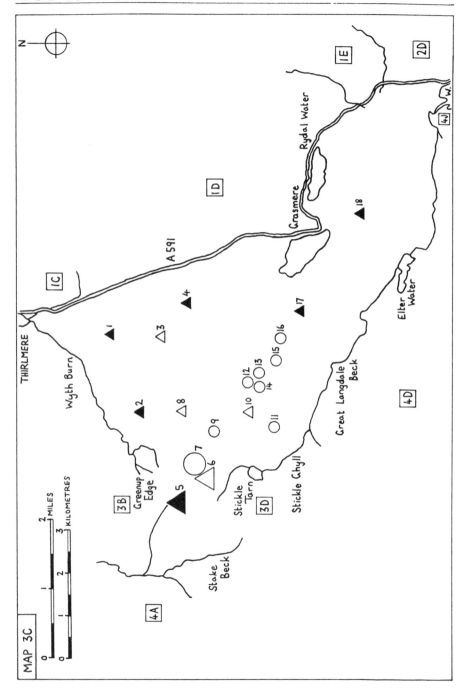

MAP 3C

TABLE 3C
THE CENTRAL FELLS - HIGH RAISE

| No. | Name | Grid ref. | Ht. | No. in order of altitude | | | OS map no. | |
				Fell	Top	AW	1:25000	1:50000
I	STEEL FELL¹	319 111	553	132	285	146	OL-NW	90
2	CALF CRAG	301 104	537x	140	313	154	OL-NW	90
3	GIBSON KNOTT	319 099	420c	-	477	198	OL-SW	90
4	HELM CRAG	327 093	405	205	504	201	OL-SE	90
5	HIGH RAISE²	281 095	762	56	82	56	OL-SW	90
6	SERGEANT MAN	286 089	730c	-	113	71	OL-SW	90
7	Codale Head	289 091	730c	-	109	-	OL-SW	90
8	TARN CRAG	303 093	550	-	297	149	OL-SW	90
9	Belles Knott	297 086	490c	-	387	-	OL-SW	90
10	BLEA RIGG	302 078	541x	-	305	151	OL-SW	90
11	Whitegill Crag	298 072	470c	-	416	-	OL-SW	90
12	Great Castle How	308 078	490c	-	388	-	OL-SW	90
13	Little Castle How	310 076	480c	-	405	-	OL-SW	90
14	Raw Pike	308 076	500	-	375	-	OL-SW	90
15	Swinescar Pike	313 072	410c	-	498	-	OL-SW	90
16	Lang How	318 071	414	-	484	-	OL-SE	90
17	SILVER HOW	325 066	395	209	524	202	OL-SE	90
18	LOUGHRIGG FELL	347 051	335	232	585	211	OL-SE	90

1. Dead Pike
2 High White Stones

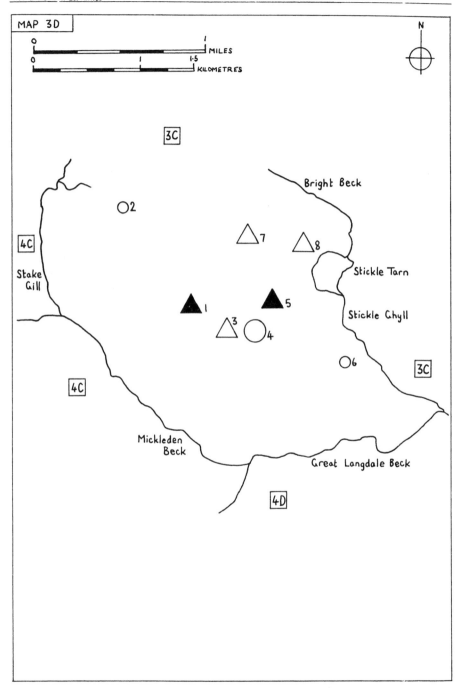

MAP 3D

0 _____ 1 MILES
0 _____ 1 ___ 1·5 KILOMETRES

N

3C

4C

Stake
Gill

Bright Beck

○2

△7   △8

Stickle Tarn

▲1   ▲5

△3   ○4   Stickle Ghyll

○6   3C

4C

Mickleden
Beck

Great Langdale Beck

4D

TABLE 3D
THE CENTRAL FELLS - THE LANGDALES

No.	Name	Grid ref.	Ht	No. in order of altitude			OS map no.	
				Fell	Top	AW	1:25000	1:50000
1	PIKE O'STICKLE	274073	709	80	131	83	OL-SW	90
2	Martcrag Moor	268083	547	-	300	-	OL-SW	90
3	LOFT CRAG	277071	680c	-	155	98	OL-SW	90
4	Thorn Crag	280071	640c	-	195	-	OL-SW	90
5	HARRISON STICKLE	282074	736	66	105	68	OL-SW	90
6	Pike How	288069	390c	-	530	-	OL-SW	90
7	THUNACAR KNOTT	279080	723	-	118	76	OL-SW	90
8	PAVEY ARK	285079	700c	-	140	89	OL-SW	90

55

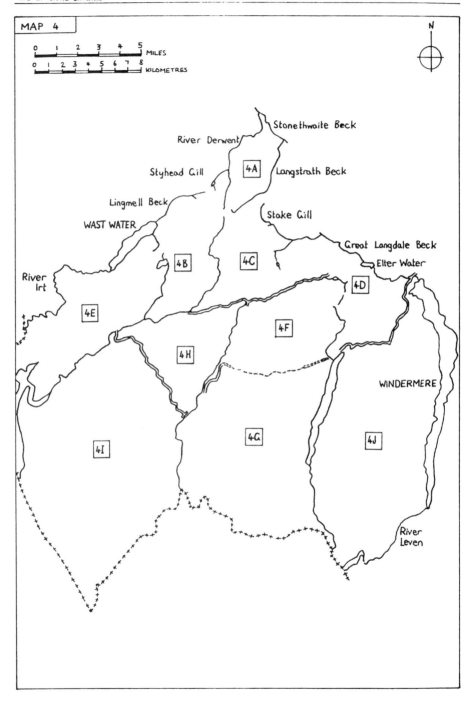

TABLE 4
THE SOUTHERN FELLS

4A	GLARAMARA AND ALLEN CRAGS
4B	THE SCAFELL PIKES
4C	BOW FELL
4D	LITTLE LANGDALE
4E	WASTWATER SCREES
4F	CONISTON
4G	WALNA SCAR AND THE DUNNERDALE FELLS
4H	HARTER FELL
4I	BLACK COMBE
4J	GRIZEDALE FOREST

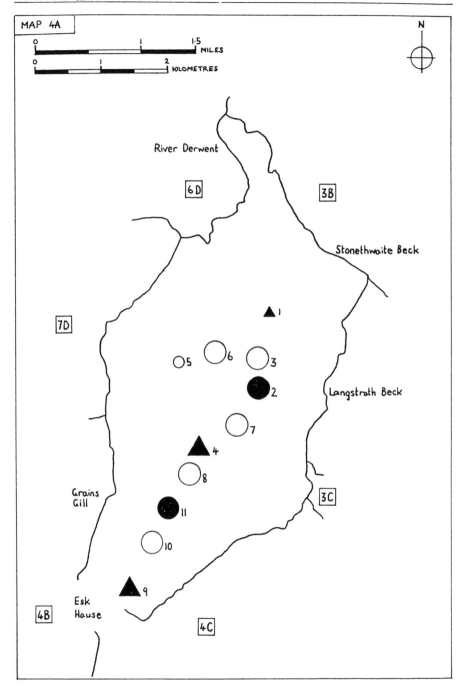

MAP 4A

0   1   1·5
MILES

0   1   2
KILOMETRES

N

River Derwent

6D

3B

Stonethwaite Beck

7D

Langstrath Beck

Grains
Gill

3C

Esk
House

4B

4C

TABLE 4A
THE SOUTHERN FELLS - GLARAMARA AND ALLEN CRAGS

No.	Name	Grid ref.	Ht.	No. in order of altitude			OS map no.	
				Fell	Top	AW	1:25000	1:50000
I	BESSYBOOT¹	258125	540c	139	309	153	OL-NW	90
2	Dovenest Crag	256114	630c	109	206	-	OL-NW	90
3	Rosthwaite Cam	256118	612	-	228	-	OL-NW	90
4	GLARAMARA	245105	783	47	65	44	OL-NW	90
5	Thornythwaite Fell	245119	574	-	263	-	OL-NW	90
6	Combe Head	250109	730c	-	110	-	OL-NW	90
7	Nameless summit (Combe Door Top)	253109	670c	-	162	-	OL-NW	90
8	Looking Steads	246102	775	-	73	-	OL-NW	90
9	ALLEN CRAGS	237085	785	45	62	42	OL-SW	90
10	Nameless summit (High House Tarn Top)	240092	684	-	150	-	OL-SW	90
11	Nameless summit (Lincomb Tarns Top)	242097	721	73	119	-	OL-SW	90

1. ROSTHWAITE FELL

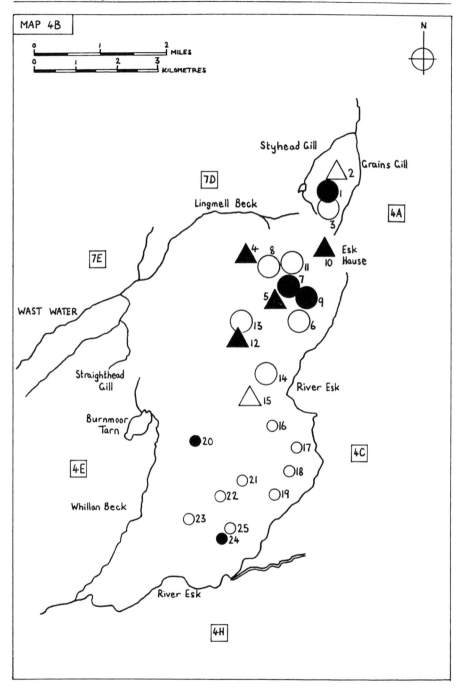

MAP 4B

MILES

KILOMETRES

N

Styhead Gill

Grains Gill

7D

Lingmell Beck

4A

7E

Esk Hause

WAST WATER

Straighthead Gill

River Esk

Burnmoor Tarn

4E

Whillan Beck

4C

River Esk

4H

60

TABLE 4B
THE SOUTHERN FELLS - THE SCAFELL PIKES

| No. | Name | Grid ref. | Ht. | No. in order of altitude | | | OS map no. | |
				Fell	Top	AW	1:25000	1:50000
1	Seathwaite Fell [1]	227097	632	108	203	-	OL-SW	89
2	SEATHWAITE FELL	229102	601	-	242	130	OL-NW	89
3	Nameless summit (Seathwaite Fell -S.Top)	228094	631	-	204	-	OL-SW	89
4	LINGMELL	209082	800c	38	53	35	OL-SW	89
5	SCAFELL PIKE	216072	978	1	1	1	OL-SW	89
6	Pen	221068	768	-	79	-	OL-SW	89
7	Broad Crag .	219076	930c	6	7	-	OL-SW	89
8	Middleboot Knotts	213081	700c	-	139	-	OL-SW	89
9	Ill Crag	223013	935	4	5	-	OL-SW	89
10	GREAT END	227084	910	7	9	5	OL-SW	89
11	Round How	220081	741	-	100	-	OL-SW	89
12	SCA FELL [2]	207065	964	2	2	2	OL-SW	89
13	Symonds Knott	208068	950c	-	3	-	OL-SW	89
14	Cam Spout Crag	214055	676	-	156	-	OL-SW	89
15	SLIGHT SIDE	210050	762x	-	83	57	OL-SW	89
16	High Scarth Crag	215044	487	-	395	-	OL-SW	89
17	Silverybield Crag	222039	395	-	525	-	OL-SW	89
18	Heron Crag	220033	350c	-	569	-	OL-SW	89
19	Brock Crag	215029	342	-	575	-	OL-SW	89
20	Great How	197040	522	154	336	-	OL-SW	89
21	Cat Crag	209031	369	-	551	-	OL-SW	89
22	Dawsonground Crags	204027	397	-	518	-	OL-SW	89
23	Peelplace Noddle	196022	300c	-	644	-	OL-SW	89
24	Goat Crag	204018	312	248	622	-	OL-SW	89
25	Bull How	206020	300c	-	642	-	OL-SW	89

1. Great Slack
2. SCAFELL

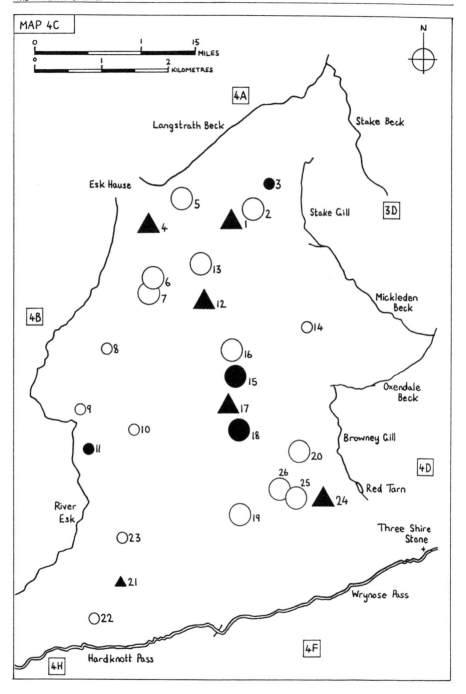

TABLE 4C
THE SOUTHERN FELLS - BOW FELL

No.	Name	Grid ref.	Ht.	No. in order of altitude			OS map no.	
				Fell	Top	AW	1:25000	1:50000
1	ROSSETT PIKE	249075	650c	100	186	115	OL-SW	89
2	Buck Pike	253078	606	-	239	-	OL-SW	89
3	Black Crags	255081	588	120	253	-	OL-SW	89
4	ESK PIKE	237075	885	12	15	11	OL-SW	89
5	Tongue Head	241080	650c	-	187	-	OL-SW	89
6	Pike de Bield	236068	810	-	43	-	OL-SW	89
7	Yeastyrigg Crags	237066	760c	-	87	-	OL-SW	89
8	High. Gait Crags	230058	570c	-	270	-	OL-SW	89
9	Scar Lathing	226049	439	-	452	-	OL-SW	89
10	Pianet Knott	234046	420c	-	478	-	OL-SW	89
11	Throstlehow Crag	227043	404	206	509	-	OL-SW	89
12	BOW FELL [1]	245064	902	8	10	6	OL-SW	89
13	Nameless summit (Bow Fell-N.Top)	245070	860c	-	22	-	OL-SW	89
14	The Band [2]	261061	568	-	273	-	OL-SW	89
15	Shelter Crags	250053	815	31	42	-	OL-SW	89
16	Nameless summit (Shelter Crags-N.Top)	249057	770c	-	77	-	OL-SW	89
17	CRINKLE CRAGS	249049	859	18	25	17	OL-SW	89
18	Crinkle Crags [3]	250046	834x	26	35	-	OL-SW	89
19	Little Stand	250034	740	-	101	-	OL-SW	89
20	Great Knott	260043	696	-	143	-	OL-SW	89
21	HARD KNOTT	232024	549	136	299	150	OL-SW	89
22	Border End	228019	522	-	335	-	OL-SW	89
23	Yew Bank	232031	499x	-	377	-	OL-SW	89
24	COLD PIKE	263036	701	84	138	88	OL-SW	89
25	Cold Pike	259036	683	-	151	-	OL-SW	89
26	Nameless summit (Cold Pike - W.Top)	256037	660c	-	172	-	OL-SW	89

1. BOWFELL
2. White Stones
3. Long Top

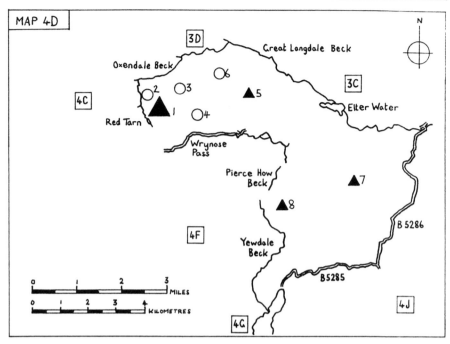

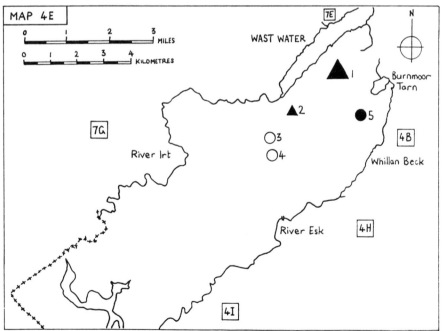

TABLE 4D
THE SOUTHERN FELLS - LITTLE LANGDALE

No.	Name	Grid ref.	Ht.	No. in order of altitude			OS map no.	
				Fell	Top	AW	1:25000	1:50000
1	PIKE OF BLISCO [1]	271042	705	82	134	86	OL-SW	90
2	Brown Howe	266047	390c	-	528	-	OL-SW	90
3	Kettle Crag	279048	390c	-	529	-	OL-SW	90
4	Blake Rigg	285039	530c	-	319	-	OL-SW	90
5	LINGMOOR FELL	303046	469	178	418	184	OL-SW	90
6	Side Pike	293053	360c	-	562	-	OL-SW	90
7	BLACK CRAG [2]	340016	323	239	603	212	OL-SE	90
8	HOLME FELL	315006	317	245	617	213	OL-SW	90

TABLE 4E
THE SOUTHERN FELLS - WASTWATER SCREES

No.	Name	Grid ref.	Ht.	No. in order of altitude			OS map no.	
				Fell	Top	AW	1:25000	1:50000
1	ILLGILL HEAD	169049	609	114	234	128	OL-SW	89
2	WHIN RIGG	152034	535	142	316	156	OL-SW	89
3	Irton Fell	144026	395	-	522	-	OL-SW	89
4	Great Bank	144019	329	-	601	-	OL-SW	89
5	Boat How	177034	337	231	584	-	OL-SW	89

1. PIKE O'BLISCO
2. Black Fell

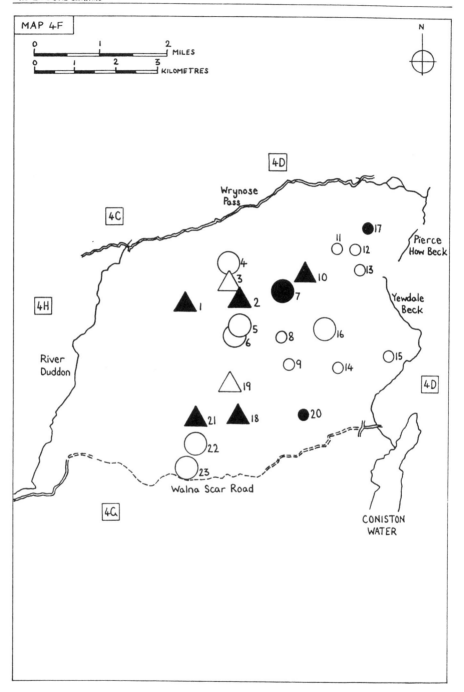

MAP 4F

0   1   2 MILES

0   1   2   3 KILOMETRES

N

4D

Wrynose Pass

4C

17

11   12

Pierce How Beck

4H

4   3

1   2   7

10

13

Yewdale Beck

River Duddon

5   6

8   16

9   14

15

4D

19

21   18

20

22

23

Walna Scar Road

4G

CONISTON WATER

TABLE 4F
THE SOUTHERN FELLS - CONISTON

No.	Name	Grid ref	Ht.	No. in order of altitude			OS map no.	
				Fell	Top	AW	1:25000	1:50000
1	GREY FRIAR	261005	770c	52	76	52	OL-SW	90
2	SWIRL HOW	273005	802x	36	50	33	OL-SW	90
3	GREAT CARRS	270009	780c	-	67	45	OL-SW	90
4	Little Carrs [1]	270014	692	-	145	-	OL-SW	90
5	Great How Crags [2]	273999	760c	-	85	-	OL-SW	96
6	Little How Crags	272997	730c	-	112	-	OL-SW	96
7	Black Sails	283007	745x	62	97	-	OL-SW	90
8	Erin Crag	283997	550c	-	290	-	OL-SW	96
9	Kennel Crag	285990	410c	-	494	-	OL-SW	96
10	WETHERLAM	288011	762	57	84	58	OL-SW	90
11	Birk Fell	296017	520c	-	339	-	OL-SW	90
12	Hawk Rigg	300017	428	-	464	-	OL-SW	90
13	Blake Rigg	301012	423	-	472	-	OL-SW	90
14	Kitty Crag	295990	435	-	456	-	OL-SW	96
15	Yewdale Crag	308993	320c	-	611	-	OL-SW	96
16	Lad Stones	292998	615x	-	226	-	OL-SW	96
17	Low Fell [3]	303022	408x	204	501	-	OL-SW	90
18	THE OLD MAN OF CONISTON [4]	272978	803	33	46	30	OL-SW	96
19	BRIM FELL	271986	796	-	55	37	OL-SW	96
20	The Bell	288979	335	234	588	-	OL-SW	96
21	DOW CRAG	262978	778	48	70	47	OL-SW	96
22	Buck Pike	262972	744	-	98	-	OL-SW	96
23	Brown Pike	261966	682	-	153	-	OL-SW	96

1. Hell Gill Pike
2. Swirl Band
3. Great Intake
4. CONISTON OLD MAN

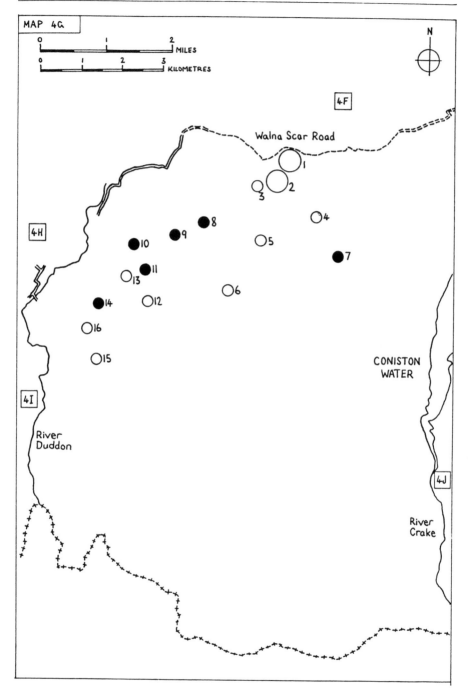

MAP 4G

0   1   2 MILES

0   1   2   3 KILOMETRES

N

4F

Walna Scar Road

4H

4I

River
Duddon

CONISTON
WATER

4J

River
Crake

TABLE 4G
THE SOUTHERN FELLS - WALNA SCAR AND THE DUNNERDALE FELLS

No.	Name	Grid ref.	Ht.	No. in order of altitude Fell	Top	AW	OS map no. 1:25000	1:50000
1	Walna Scar	258963	621	-	218	-	OL-SW	96
2	White Maiden	254957	608	-	237	-	OL-SW	96
3	White Pike	249956	598	·	245	-	OL-SW	96
4	High Pike Haw	264949	354	-	567	-	OL-SW	96
5	Broughton Moor	251943	410c	-	489	-	OL-SW	96
6	The Knott	243932	332x	-	593	-	OL-SW	96
7	Banks	269940	303	253	638	-	OL-SW	96
8	Pikes	238947	469	179	419	-	OL-SW	96
9	Caw	230945	529	145	321	-	OL-SW	96
10	Brock Barrow	220943	343	225	572	-	OL-SW	96
11	Fox Haw	223936	385	215	536	-	OL-SW	96
12	Nameless summit (Raven's Crag)	224929	361	-	558	-	OL-SW	96
13	Nameless summit (Park Head Road Top)	218935	307	-	632	-	OL-SW	96
14	Stickle Pike	212927	375	217	545	-	OL-SW	96
15	Great Stickle	212916	305	-	636	-	OL-SW	96
16	Tarn Hill	209923	310c	-	630	-	OL-SW	96

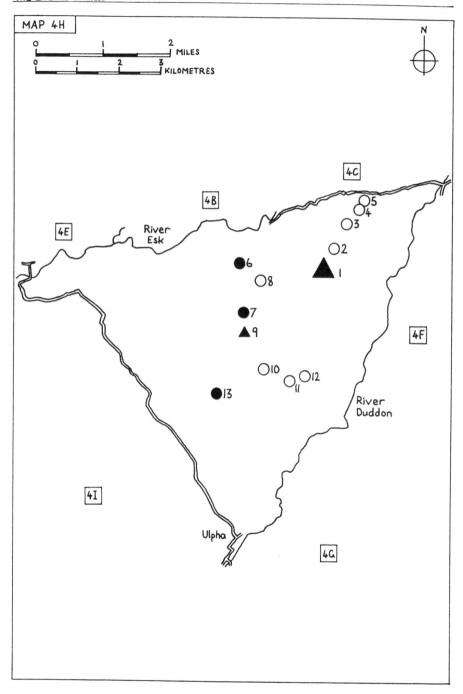

TABLE 4H
THE SOUTHERN FELLS - HARTER FELL

| No. | Name | Grid ref. | Ht. | No. in order of altitude | | | OS map no. | |
				Fell	Top	AW	1:25000	1:50000
1	HARTER FELL	219997	653	98	182	112	OL-SW	96
2	Demming Crags	222002	525	-	329	-	OL-SW	89
3	Horsehow Crags	224008	433	-	458	-	OL-SW	89
4	Nameless summit (Peathill Crag - S.Top)	227012	404	-	508	-	OL-SW	89
5	Peathill Crag	228013	400c	-	515	-	OL-SW	89
6	Kepple Crag	199999	328	238	602	-	OL-SW	96
7	Crook Crag .	200987	469	177	417	-	OL-SW	96
8	Dow Crag	204995	404	-	506	-	OL-SW	96
9	GREEN CRAG	200983	489	169	391	176	OL-SW	96
10	White How	205975	444	-	445	-	OL-SW	96
11	Iron Crag	211972	408	-	500	-	OL-SW	96
12	Wallowbarrow Heald	215973	370c	-	549	-	OL-SW	96
13	Great Worm Crag	194969	427	196	466	-	OL-SW	96

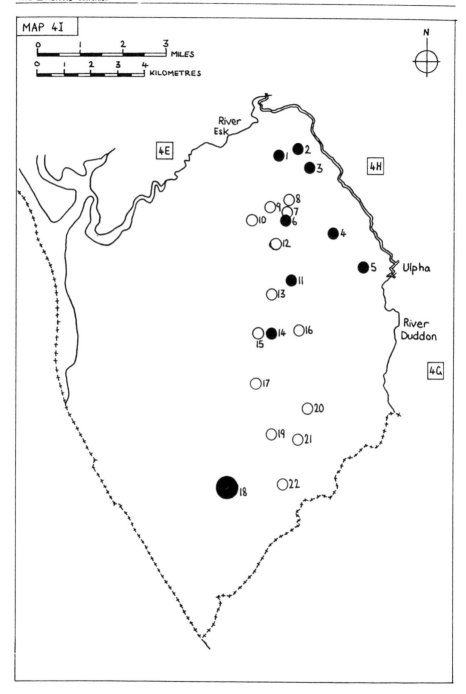

MAP 4I

N

River Esk

4E

4H

Ulpha

River Duddon

4G

TABLE 4I
THE SOUTHERN FELLS - BLACK COMBE

No.	Name	Grid ref.	Ht.	No. in order of altitude Fell	Top	AW	OS map no. 1:25000	1:50000
1	Water Crag	154975	305	252	637	-	OL-SW	96
2	Rough Crag	161978	319	244	614	-	OL-SW	96
3	Seat How	165971	311	250	627	-	OL-SW	96
4	Hesk Fell	176947	477	176	408	-	OL-SW	96
5	The Pike	186934	370	219	550	-	OL-SW	96
6	Yoadcastle	157952	494	165	383	-	OL-SW	96
7	Woodend Height	157954	480c	-	406	-	OL-SW	96
8	Rowantree How	157959	400c	-	517	-	OL-SW	96
9	White Pike	151956	442	-	447	-	OL-SW	96
10	The Knott	144951	331	-	595	-	OL-SW	96
11	Whitfell	159930	573	125	265	-	OL-SW	96
12	Stainton Pike	153943	498	-	378	-	OL-SW	96
13	Burn Moor	151924	543	-	303	-	OL-SW	96
14	Buck Barrow	152910	549	135	298	-	OL-SW	96
15	Kinmont Buck Barrow	147910	535	-	315	-	OL-SW	96
16	Plough Fell	162912	448	-	438	-	OL-SW	96
17	Stoneside Hill	146893	422x	-	474	-	PF625	96
18	Black Combe	135855	600	116	244	-	PF625	96
19	Stoupdale Crags	151874	472	-	412	-	PF625	96
20	Raven Crag	166883	376	-	542	-	PF625	96
21	Gray Stones	161873	396	-	520	-	PF625	96
22	White Hall Knott	156855	311	-	628	-	PF625	96

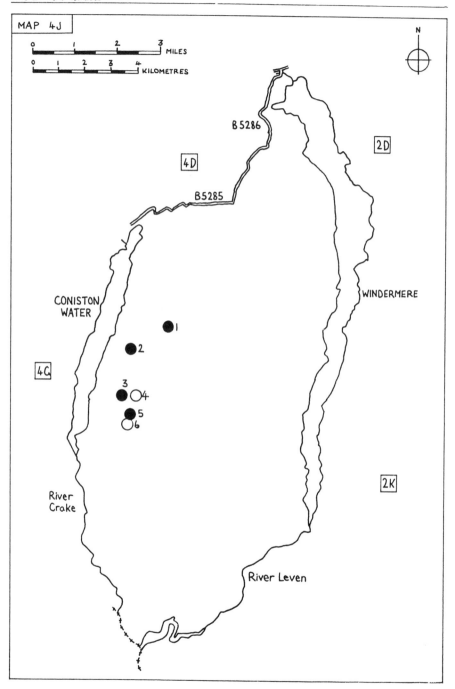

MAP 4J

0   1   2   3 MILES

0   1   2   3   4 KILOMETRES

N

B 5286

4D

2D

B 5285

CONISTON
WATER

WINDERMERE

● 1

● 2

4G

3 ● ○ 4

● 5

○ 6

River
Crake

2K

River Leven

TABLE 4J
THE SOUTHERN FELLS - GRIZEDALE FOREST

| No. | Name | Grid ref. | Ht. | No. in order of altitude | | | OS map no. | |
				Fell	Top	AW	1:25000	1:50000
1	Carron Crag¹	325943	314	246	620	-	OL·SE	96
2	Park Crags	311935	302	255	641	-	OL·SW	96
3	Top O'Selside	309919	335	235	589	-	OL·SW	96
4	Heel Toe Hill	313919	320c	-	610	-	OL·SW	96
5	Arnsbarrow Hill	311911	322	240	604	-	OL·SW	96
6	Nameless summit (Arnsbarrow Hill - S.Top)	310908	316	-	618	-	OL·SW	96

1. Grizedale Forest

75

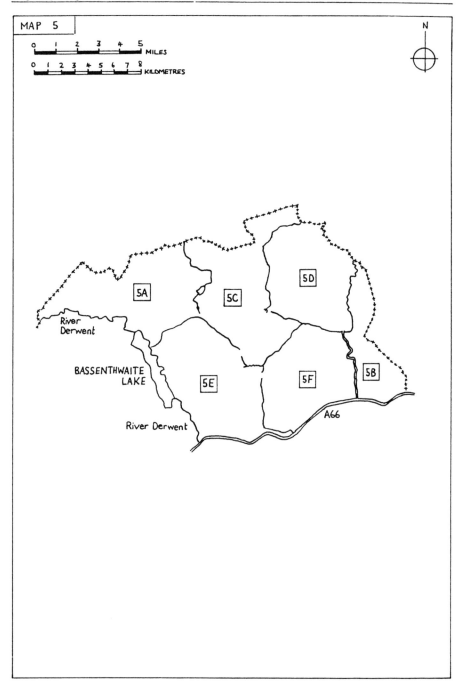

TABLE 5
THE NORTHERN FELLS

5A	BINSEY
5B	EYCOTT HILL
5C	ULDALE FELLS
5D	CALDBECK FELLS
5E	SKIDDAW
5F	BLENCATHRA

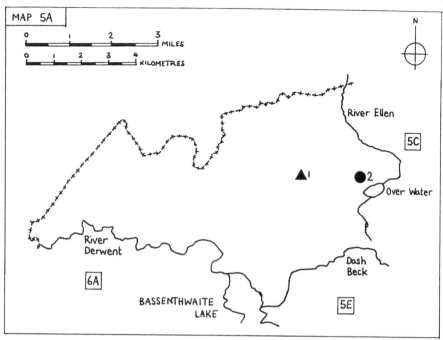

MAP 5A

0 1 2 3 MILES
0 1 2 3 4 KILOMETRES

N

River Ellen

5C

▲1 ●2

Over Water

River
Derwent

6A

Dash
Beck

BASSENTHWAITE
LAKE

5E

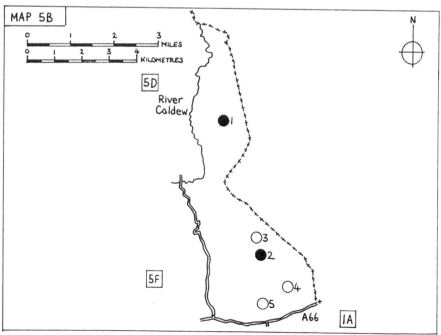

MAP 5B

0 1 2 3 MILES
0 1 2 3 4 KILOMETRES

N

5D

River
Caldew

●1

○3
●2

5F

○4

○5

A66 1A

TABLE 5A
THE NORTHERN FELLS - BINSEY

| No. | Name | Grid ref. | Ht. | No. in order of altitude | | | OS map no. | |
				Fell	Top	AW	1:25000	1:50000
1	BINSEY	225355	447	187	439	190	PF576	90
2	Latrigg	246355	322x	241	605	-	PF576	90

TABLE 5B
THE NORTHERN FELLS - EYCOTT HILL

| No. | Name | Grid ref. | Ht. | No. in order of altitude | | | OS map no. | |
				Fell	Top	AW	1:25000	1:50000
1	Hutton Roof	373341	308	251	631	-	PF576	90
2	Eycott Hill	386295	345	224	570	-	OL-NE	90
3	Little Eycott Hill	385301	330c	-	598	-	PF576	90
4	Greenah Crag	396284	303	-	639	-	OL-NE	90
5	Lofshaw Hill	387278	312	-	623	-	OL-NE	90

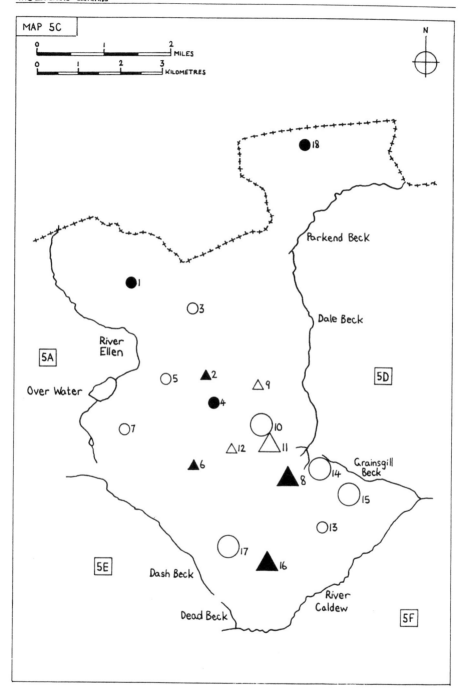

MAP 5C

N

0 ___ 1 ___ 2 MILES
0 __ 1 __ 2 __ 3 KILOMETRES

●18

Parkend Beck

●1

○3

Dale Beck

River
Ellen

5A

Over Water

5D

○5 ▲2

△9

●4

○7

○10

△12 △11

▲6

▲8 ○14 Grainsgill Beck

○15

○13

○17 ▲16

5E Dash Beck

River Caldew

Dead Beck

5F

TABLE 5C
THE NORTHERN FELLS - ULDALE FELLS

No.	Name	Grid ref.	Ht.	No. in order of altitude Fell	Top	AW	OS map no. 1:25000	1:50000
I	Green How [1]	258375	321x	242	606	-	PF576	90
2	LONGLANDS FELL	276354	483	173	400	179	PF576	90
3	Mickle Rigg	273369	316	-	619	-	PF576	90
4	Lowthwaite Fell	278347	509	160	360	-	PF576	90
5	Nameless summit (Lowthwaite Fell -W.Top)	267353	311	-	626	-	PF576	90
6	GREAT COCKUP	273333	526	148	327	159	PF576	90
7	Castle How	257342	305	-	635	-	PF576	90
8	KNOTT	296330	710	79	129	82	PF576	90
9	BRAE FELL	289352	586	-	255	134	PF576	90
10	Little Sca Fell	290342	630c	-	208	-	PF576	90
11	GREAT SCA FELL	291339	651	-	184	114	PF576	90
12	MEAL FELL	283337	550	-	296	148	PF576	90
13	Pike	303320	590c	-	250	-	PF576	90
14	Little Lingy Hill	302334	600c	-	243	-	PF576	90
15	Coomb Height	310327	627x	-	212	-	PF576	90
16	GREAT CALVA	291312	690	87	149	96	PF576	90
17	Little Calva	282315	642	-	191	-	PF576	90
18	Faulds Brow	299407	343	226	573	-	PF567	85

1. Aughertree Fell

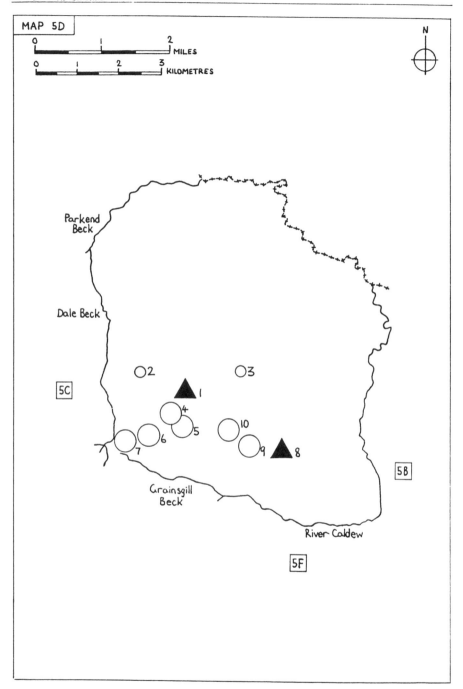

MAP 5D

N

0   1   2 MILES

0   1   2   3 KILOMETRES

Parkend Beck

Dale Beck

2

3

5C

1

4

5

10

6

7

9

8

5B

Grainsgill Beck

River Caldew

5F

TABLE 5D
THE NORTHERN FELLS - CALDBECK FELLS

| No. | Name | Grid ref. | Ht. | No. in order of altitude | | | OS map no. | |
				Fell	Top	AW	1:25000	1:50000
1	HIGH PIKE	319350	658	95	176	107	PF576	90
2	Birk Hill	308355	501	-	369	-	PF576	90
3	West Fell	332355	511	-	353	-	PF576	90
4	Hare Stones	316344	627	-	213	-	PF576	90
5	Drygill Head	318342	620c	-	219	-	PF576	90
6	Great Lingy Hill	310340	616	-	224	-	PF576	90
7	Iron Crag	304339	609	-	235	-	PF576	90
8	CARROCK FELL	342336	660c	93	171	105	PF576	90
9	Round Knott	334337	603	-	241	-	PF576	90
10	Miton Hill	329341	607		238	-	PF576	90

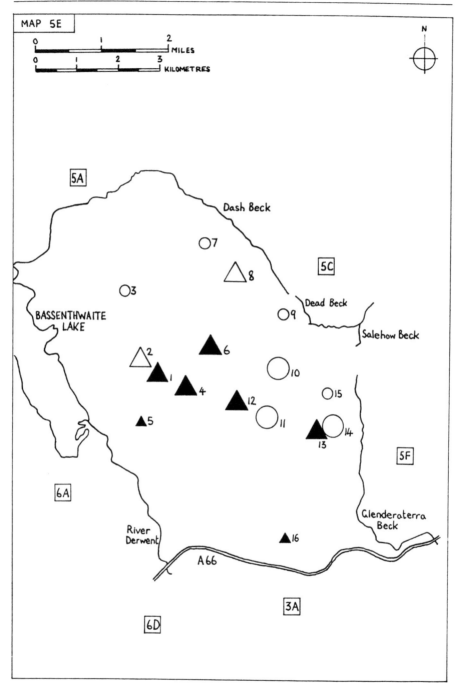

MAP 5E

0   1   2
MILES
0   1   2   3
KILOMETRES

N

5A

Dash Beck

○7

△8

5C

○3

Dead Beck

BASSENTHWAITE
LAKE

○9

Salehow Beck

▲6

△2

▲1

▲4

○10

▲5

▲12

○15

○11

▲13 ○14

5F

6A

Glenderaterra
Beck

River
Derwent

▲16

A66

3A

6D

TABLE 5E
THE NORTHERN FELLS - SKIDDAW

No.	Name	Grid ref.	Ht.	No. in order of altitude			OS map no.	
				Fell	Top	AW	1:25000	1:50000
1	LONG SIDE [1]	249284	734	68	107	70	OI-NW	90
2	ULLOCK PIKE	244288	690c	-	148	95	OI-NW	90
3	Watches	241304	333	-	591	-	PF576	90
4	CARL SIDE	255281	746	61	96	64	OI-NW	90
5	DODD	244273	502	162	367	174	OI-NW	90
6	SKIDDAW	260291	931	5	6	4	OI-NW	90
7	Cockup	259314	505	-	364	-	PF576	90
8	BAKESTALL	266307	673	-	158	100	PF576	90
9	Hare Crag	277299	538	-	312	-	OI-NW	90
10	Sale How	276286	666	-	167	-	OI-NW	90
11	Jenkin Hill	274275	730c	-	111	-	OI-NW	90
12	LITTLE MAN	267278	865	16	20	15	OI-NW	90
13	LONSCALE FELL	285271	715	77	125	80	OI-NW	90
14	Nameless summit (Lonscale Fell - E.Top)	289273	703	-	136	-	OI-NW	90
15	Burnt Horse	288280	570	-	271	-	OI-NW	90
16	LATRIGG	279247	368	220	552	206	OI-NW	90

1. Longside Edge

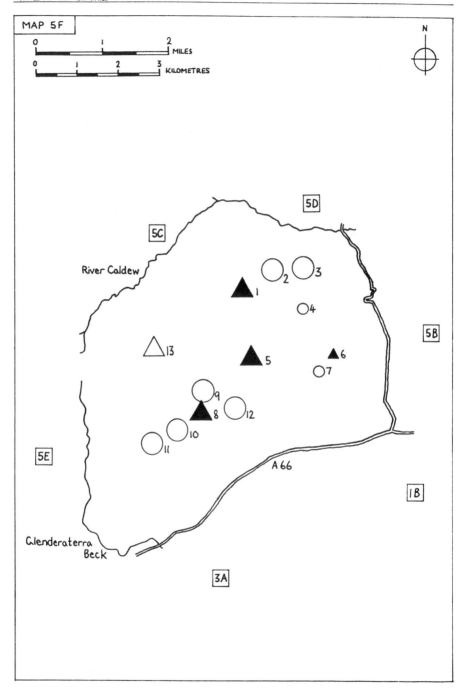

MAP 5F

0   1   2 MILES

0   1   2   3 KILOMETRES

N

5D

5C

River Caldew

5B

13

5E

A 66

Glenderaterra
Beck

3A

1B

TABLE 5F
THE NORTHERN FELLS - BLENCATHRA

No.	Name	Grid ref.	Ht.	No. in order of altitude Fell	Top	AW	OS map no. 1:25000	1:50000
1	BOWSCALE FELL	333305	702	83	137	87	PF576	90
2	Nameless summit (Bowscale Fell - E.Top)	341311	660c	-	169	-	PF576	90
3	Nameless summit (Bowscale Fell - Far E.Top)	348311	604	-	240	-	PF576	90
4	The Tongue	348302	553	-	288	-	PF576	90
5	BANNERDALE CRAGS	335290	683	88	152	97	OL-NE	90
6	SOUTHER FELL	355291	522	155	337	163	OL-NE	90
7	Nameless summit (Souther Fell - S.Top)	352287	510c	-	357	-	OL-NE	90
8	BLENCATHRA [1]	323277	868	15	19	14	OL-NE	90
9	Foule Crag [2]	324283	845	-	30	-	OL-NE	90
10	Gategill Fell	318274	851	-	29	-	OL-NE	90
11	Knowe Crags [3]	312270	804	-	45	-	OL-NE	90
12	Scales Fell [4]	332279	682	-	154	-	OL-NE	90
13	MUNGRISDALE COMMON	312292	633	-	201	121	OL-NE	90

1. Saddleback or Hallsfell Top
2. Atkinson Pike or Tarn Crags
3. Blease Fell
4. Doddick Fell

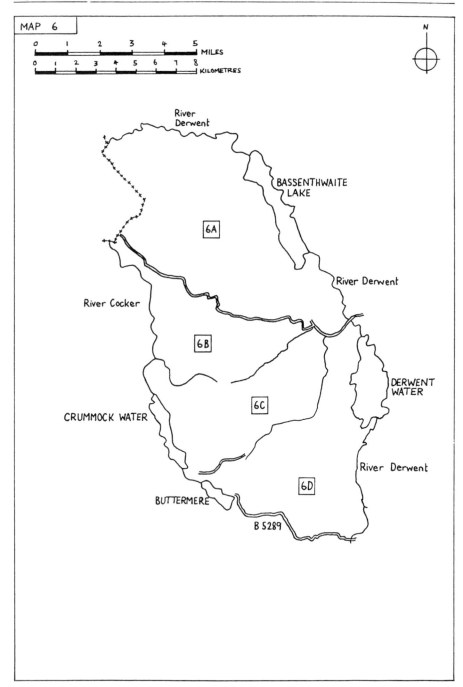

TABLE 6
THE NORTH WESTERN FELLS

6A	WHINLATTER
6B	GRISEDALE PIKE
6C	GRASMOOR
6D	NEWLANDS

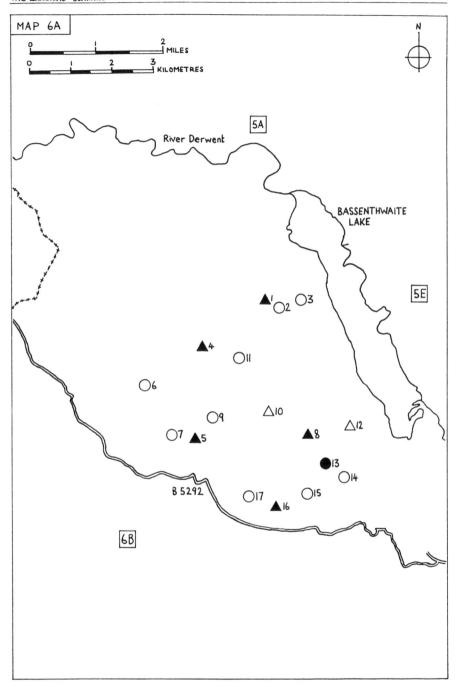

MAP 6A

0   1   2 MILES

0   1   2   3 KILOMETRES

N

River Derwent

5A

BASSENTHWAITE LAKE

5E

BassenthwaiteLake

B 5292

6B

TABLE 6A
THE NORTH WESTERN FELLS - WHINLATTER

No.	Name	Grid ref.	Ht.	No. in order of altitude			OS map no	
				Fell	Top	AW	1:25000	1:50000
1	SALE FELL	194297	359	222	564	208	OL-NW	89
2	Rivings	198294	335	-	586	-	OL-NW	89
3	Lowthwaite	203297	345	-	571	-	OL-NW	89
4	LING FELL	180286	373	218	547	205	OL-NW	89
5	GRAYSTONES	178264	456	182	429	187	OL-NW	89
6	Embleton High Common	167274	319	-	613	-	OL-NW	89
7	Kirk Fell	173266	438	-	453	-	OL-NW	89
8	LORD'S SEAT	204266	552	134	289	147	OL-NW	89
9	Widow House	183269	404	-	510	-	OL-NW	89
10	BROOM FELL	196270	511	-	352	169	OL-NW	89
11	Burthwaite Heights	189283	318	-	616	-	OL-NW	89
12	BARF	214268	468x	-	420	185	OL-NW	89
13	Ullister Hill	209260	525	150	330	-	OL-NW	89
14	Seat How	213256	496x	-	380	-	OL-NW	89
15	Tarbarrel Moss	206253	493	-	386	-	OL-NW	89
16	WHINLATTER	197249	525	151	331	160	OL-NW	89
17	Brown How	191251	517	-	343	-	OL-NW	89

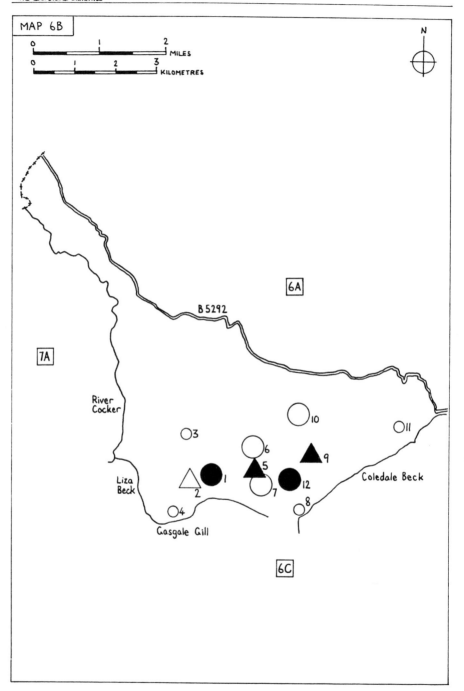

TABLE 6B
THE NORTH WESTERN FELLS - GRISEDALE PIKE

| No. | Name | Grid ref. | Ht. | No. in order of altitude | | | OS map no. | |
				Fell	Top	AW	1:25000	1:50000
1	Nameless summit (Gasgale Crags)[1]	175221	719	75	122	-	OL-NW	89
2	WHITESIDE	170219	707	-	132	84	OL-NW	89
3	Dodd	169231	454	-	432	-	OL-NW	89
4	Whin Ben	166213	413	-	485	-	OL-NW	89
5	HOPEGILL HEAD	186222	770	53	78	53	OL-NW	89
6	Ladyside Pike	185227	703	-	135	-	OL-NW	89
7	Sand Hill	187219	756	-	90	-	OL-NW	89
8	Force Crag	196213	475	-	410	-	OL-NW	89
9	GRISEDALE PIKE	198225	791	43	59	40	OL-NW	89
10	Hobcarton End	195235	634	-	200	~	OL-NW	89
11	Kinn	219232	374	-	546	-	OL-NW	89
12	Hobcarton Crag	194220	739	64	102	-	OL-NW	89

1. Whiteside -E.Top

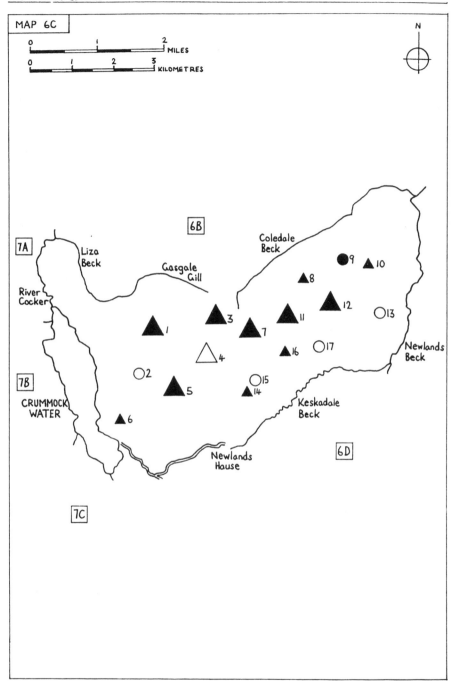

MAP 6C

0   1   2
|—————|—————| MILES

0   1   2   3
|————|————|————| KILOMETRES

N

7A

Liza
Beck

6B

Coledale
Beck

Gasgale
Gill

River
Cocker

●9   ▲10

▲8

▲12

▲1   ▲3   ◯13

▲7   ▲11

△4   ▲16   ◯17

◯2   Newlands
Beck

7B   ▲5   ◯15
                    ▲14

CRUMMOCK
WATER   ▲6   Keskadale
Beck

6D

Newlands
House

7C

TABLE 6C
THE NORTH WESTERN FELLS - GRASMOOR

No.	Name	Grid ref.	Ht.	No. in order of altitude			OS map no.	
				Fell	Top	AW	1:25000	1:50000
1	GRASMOOR	175203	852	21	28	20	OL-NW	89
2	Lad Hows	172193	426	-	469	-	OL-NW	89
3	CRAG HILL'	193204	839	25	34	24	OL-NW	89
4	WANDOPE	188197	772	-	75	51	OL-NW	89
5	WHITELESS PIKE	180190	660	94	175	106	OL-NW	89
6	RANNERDALE KNOTTS	167182	355	223	566	209	OL-NW	89
7	SAIL	198203	773	51	74	50	OL-NW	89
8	OUTERSIDE	211215	568	127	272	142	OL-NW	89
9	Stile End	221219	447	189	441	-	OL-NW	89
10	BARROW	227218	455	183	430	188	OL-NW	89
11	SCAR CRAGS	208206	672	90	160	101	OL-NW	89
12	CAUSEY PIKE	219209	637	105	197	119	OL-NW	89
13	Rowling End	229207	433	-	459	-	OL-NW	89
14	KNOTT RIGG	197189	556	131	283	145	OL-NW	89
15	Nameless summit (Knott Rigg - N.Top)	200192	546	-	301	-	OL-NW	89
16	ARD CRAGS	207198	581	122	257	136	OL-NW	89
17	Aikin Knott	215199	470c	-	413	-	OL-NW	89

1. EEL CRAG

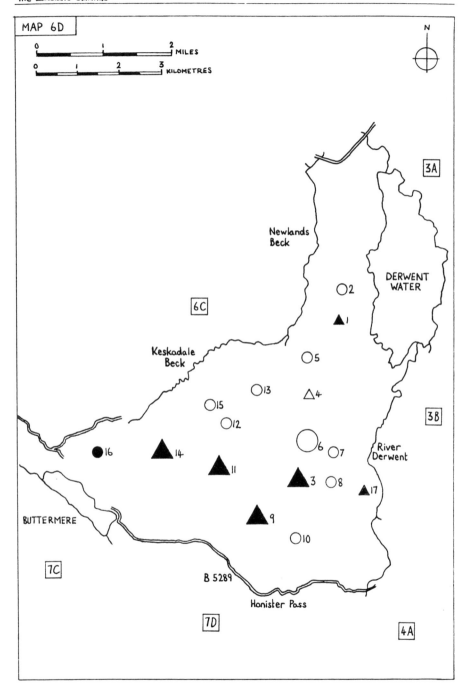

MAP 6D

N

0   1   2 MILES

0   1   2   3 KILOMETRES

3A

Newlands
Beck

DERWENT
WATER

○2

▲1

6C

Keskadale
Beck

○5

○13 △4

○15

3B

○12

○16 ▲14 ○6 ○7 River
Derwent

▲11 ▲3 ○8 ▲17

BUTTERMERE ▲9 ○10

7C

B 5289

Honister Pass

7D

4A

TABLE 6D
THE NORTH WESTERN FELLS - NEWLANDS

No.	Name	Grid ref.	Ht.	No. in order of altitude			OS map no.	
				Fell	Top	AW	1:25000	1:50000
1	CAT BELLS [1]	244199	451	186	434	189	OL-NW	89
2	Skelgill Bank	245206	338	-	583	-	OL-NW	89
3	HIGH SPY	234162	653x	99	183	113	OL-NW	89
4	MAIDEN MOOR	237182	576	-	259	138	OL-NW	89
5	High Crags	237190	412	-	486	-	OL-NW	89
6	Blea Crag	236171	630c	-	205	-	OL-NW	89
7	Nitting Haws	243168	410c	-	495	-	OL-NW	89
8	Low Scawdel	243161	521	-	338	-	OL-NW	89
9	DALE HEAD	223153	753	60	93	63	OL-NW	89
10	High Scawdel	233149	550c	-	292	-	OL-NW	89
11	HINDSCARTH	216165	727	70	115	73	OL-NW	89
12	High Crags	217175	529	-	322	-	OL-NW	89
13	Scope End	224183	410c	-	496	-	OL-NW	89
14	ROBINSON	202169	737	65	104	67	OL-NW	89
15	High Snab Bank [2]	213179	430c	-	461	-	OL-NW	89
16	High Snockrigg	187169	526	149	328	-	OL-NW	89
17	CASTLE CRAG	250160	290	257	646	214	OL-NW	89

1. CATBELLS
2. Blea Crags

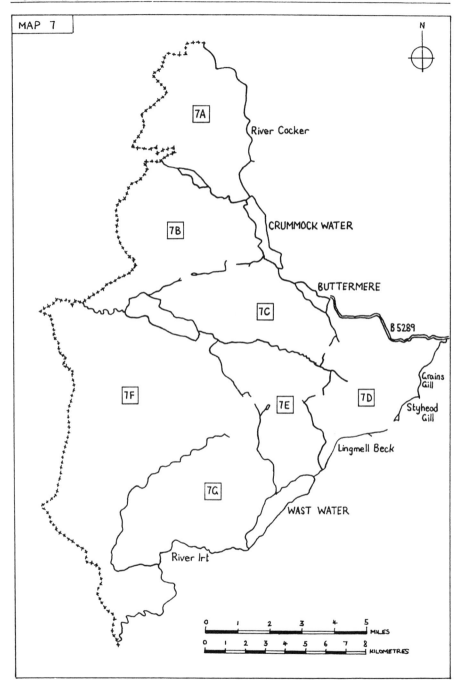

MAP 7

N

7A

River Cocker

7B

CRUMMOCK WATER

BUTTERMERE

7C

B 5289

Crains Gill

7F

7E

7D

Styhead Gill

Lingmell Beck

7G

WAST WATER

River Irt

0   1   2   3   4   5
MILES

0 1 2 3 4 5 6 7 8
KILOMETRES

TABLE 7
THE WESTERN FELLS

7A	FELLBARROW
7B	THE LOWESWATER FELLS
7C	BUTTERMERE
7D	GREAT GABLE
7E	PILLAR
7F	ENNERDALE
7G	NETHER WASDALE

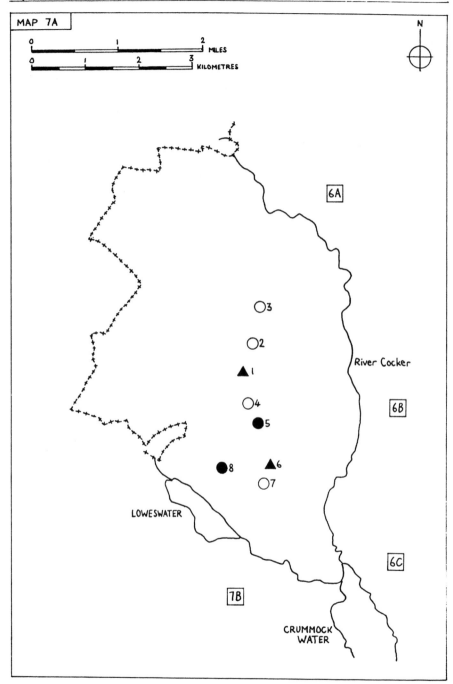

MAP 7A

0   1   2 MILES
0   1   2   3 KILOMETRES

N

6A

○3

○2

▲1

○4

●5

●8   ▲6

○7

River Cocker

6B

6C

LOWESWATER

7B

CRUMMOCK
WATER

TABLE 7A
THE WESTERN FELLS - FELLBARROW

No.	Name	Grid ref.	Ht.	No. in order of altitude			OS map no.	
				Fell	Top	AW	1:25000	1:50000
1	FELLBARROW	132242	416	200	482	199	OL NW	89
2	Hatteringill Head	134248	385	-	537	-	OL NW	89
3	Nameless summit (Whin Fell)	135255	306	-	633	-	OL NW	89
4	Smithy Fell	133237	390c	-	531	-	OL NW	89
5	Sourfoot Fell	135233	410c	203	497	-	OL NW	89
6	LOW FELL	137226	423	199	473	196	OL NW	89
7	Nameless summit (Low Fell)	136223	412	-	487	-	OL NW	89
8	Darling Fell	128225	391	211	527	-	OL NW	89

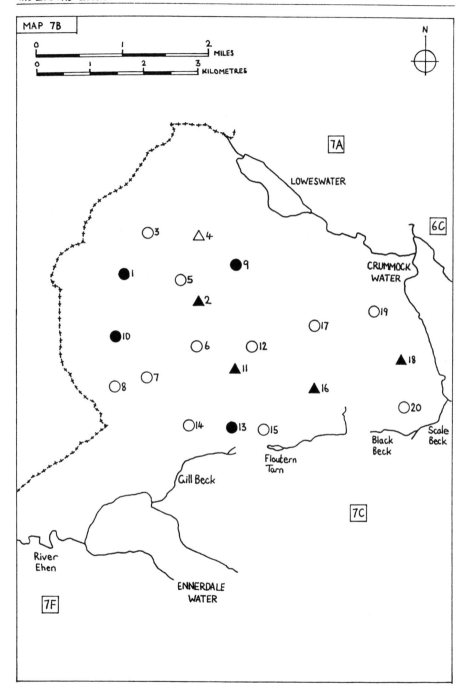

MAP 7B

0 1 2 MILES

0 1 2 3 KILOMETRES

N

7A

LOWESWATER

6C

3 △4

9

1

5

▲2

CRUMMOCK WATER

19

17

10

6 12

18

8 7

11

16

14 13 15

20

Floutern Tarn

Black Beck

Scale Beck

Gill Beck

7C

River Ehen

ENNERDALE WATER

7F

TABLE 7B
THE WESTERN FELLS - THE LOWESWATER FELLS

| No. | Name | Grid ref. | Ht. | No. in order of altitude | | | OS map no. | |
				Fell	Top	AW	1:25000	1:50000
1	High Hows	096202	313	247	621	–	OL·NW	89
2	BLAKE FELL	110197	573	124	264	140	OL·NW	89
3	Owsen Fell	101209	409	–	499	–	OL·NW	89
4	BURNBANK FELL	110209	475	–	409	183	OL·NW	89
5	Sharp Knott	107201	482	–	403	–	OL·NW	89
6	High Pen	110189	475	–	411	–	OL·NW	89
7	Godworth	101183	365	–	555	–	OL·NW	89
8	Kelton Fell	095181	311	–	625	–	OL·NW	89
9	Carling Knott	117203	544	137	302	–	OL·NW	89
10	Knock Murton	095191	447	188	440	–	OL·NW	89
11	GAVEL FELL	117185	526	147	326	158	OL·NW	89
12	Nameless summit (Gavel Fell N.Top)	120189	488	–	392	–	OL·NW	89
13	Nameless summit (Banna Fell - E.Top)	116174	456	181	428	–	OL·NW	89
14	Banna Fell	109175	411	–	488	–	OL·NW	89
15	Floutern Cop	122174	451	–	436	–	OL·NW	89
16	HEN COMB	132181	509	159	359	171	OL·NW	89
17	Little Dodd	132192	360c	–	560	–	OL·NW	89
18	MELLBREAK	149186	512	157	351	168	OL·NW	89
19	Nameless summit (Mellbreak N.Top)	143195	509	–	361	–	OL·NW	89
20	Scale Knott	149178	338	–	581	–	OL·NW	89

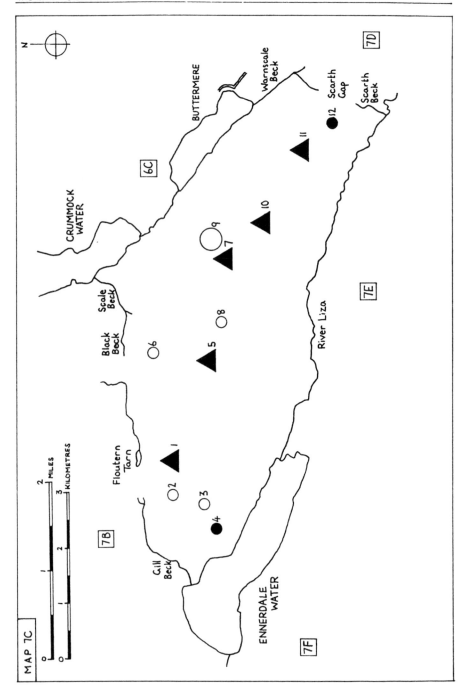

MAP 7C

TABLE 7C
THE WESTERN FELLS - BUTTERMERE

No.	Name	Grid ref.	Ht.	No. in order of altitude			OS map no.	
				Fell	Top	AW	1:25000	1:50000
1	GREAT BORNE	124164	616	112	223	126	OL-NW	89
2	Herdus	118163	562	-	277	-	OL-NW	89
3	Brown How	116158	320c	-	608	-	OL-NW	89
4	Bowness Knott	112155	333	236	590	-	OL-NW	89
5	STARLING DODD	142158	633	107	202	122	OL-NW	89
6	Gale Fell	144168	499	-	376	-	OL-NW	89
7	RED PIKE	161154	755	59	91	62	OL-NW	89
8	Little Dodd	149155	590	-	252	-	OL-NW	89
9	Dodd	164157	641	-	192	-	OL-NW	89
10	HIGH STILE	170148	807	32	44	29	OL-NW	89
11	HIGH CRAG	180140	744	63	99	65	OL-NW	89
12	Seat	186134	561	129	279	-	OL-NW	89

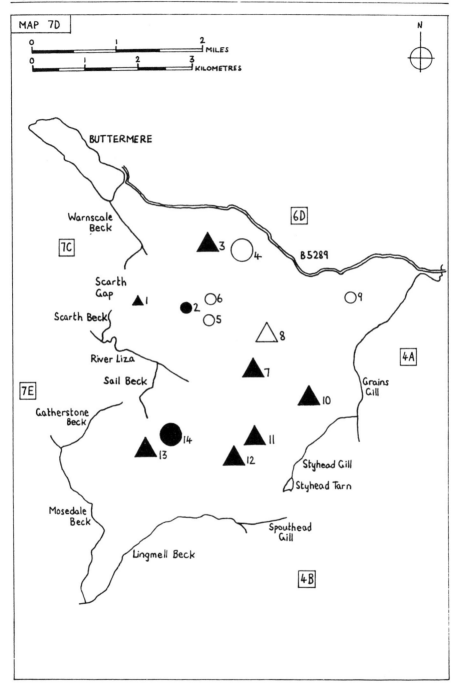

MAP 7D

0   1   2 MILES

0   1   2   3 KILOMETRES

N

BUTTERMERE

Warnscale
Beck

6D

7C

Scarth
Gap

B5289

Scarth Beck

River Liza

Sail Beck

4A

7E

Grains
Gill

Gatherstone
Beck

Styhead Gill

Styhead Tarn

Mosedale
Beck

Spouthead
Gill

Lingmell Beck

4B

TABLE 7D
THE WESTERN FELLS - GREAT GABLE

| No. | Name | Grid ref. | Ht. | No. in order of altitude | | | OS map no. | |
				Fell	Top	AW	1:25000	1:50000
1	HAY STACKS[1]	193131	597	117	246	131	OL-NW	89
2	Green Crag	203131	528	146	324	-	OL-NW	89
3	FLEETWITH PIKE	206142	648	101	188	116	OL-NW	89
4	Honister Crag[2]	213141	630c	-	207	-	OL-NW	89
5	Great Round How	207128	554	-	284	-	OL-NW	89
6	Little Round How	207132	494	-	382	-	OL-NW	89
7	BRANDRETH	215119	715	76	124	79	OL-NW	89
8	GREY KNOTTS	217126	697	-	142	91	OL-NW	89
9	Seatoller Fell	233132	461x	-	425	-	OL-NW	89
10	BASE BROWN	225115	646	102	189	117	OL-NW	89
11	GREEN GABLE	215107	801	37	52	34	OL-NW	89
12	GREAT GABLE	211103	899	9	11	7	OL-NW	89
13	KIRK FELL	195105	802	35	49	32	OL-NW	89
14	Nameless summit (Kirk Fell - E. Top)	199107	787	44	61	-	OL-NW	89

1. HAYSTACKS
2. Black Star

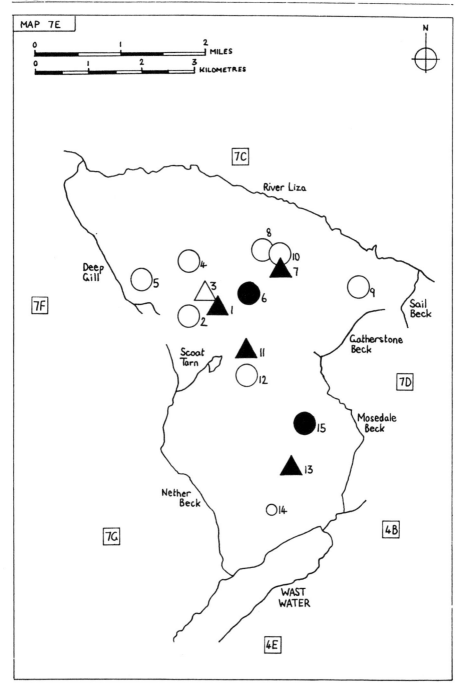

MAP 7E

0   1   2   MILES

0   1   2   3   KILOMETRES

N

7C

River Liza

8

4

10

7

Deep Gill

5

3

1

6

9

Sail Beck

7F

2

Catherstone Beck

Scoat Tarn

11

12

7D

15

Mosedale Beck

13

Nether Beck

14

4B

7G

WAST WATER

4E

TABLE 7E
THE WESTERN FELLS - PILLAR

| No. | Name | Grid ref. | Ht. | No. in order of altitude | | | OS map no. | |
				Fell	Top	AW	1:25000	1:50000
I	LITTLE SCOAT FELL'	160114	841	23	32	22	OL-NW	89
2	Great Scoat Fell	155112	802	-	47	-	OL-NW	89
3	STEEPLE	157117	819	-	41	28	OL-NW	89
4	Long Crag	154122	650c	-	185	-	OL-NW	89
5	Tewit How	145119	610	-	233	-	OL-NW	89
6	Black Crag	166117	828	27	36	-	OL-NW	89
7	PILLAR	171121	892	10	12	8	OL-NW	89
8	White Pike	169124	782	-	66	-	OL-NW	89
9	Looking Stead	186118	627	-	214	-	OL-NW	89
10	Pillar Rock	172124	780c	-	69	-	OL-NW	89
II	RED PIKE	165106	826	29	38	26	OL-NW	89
12	Black Crag	166101	801	-	51	-	OL-NW	89
13	YEWBARROW	173085	628	III	211	123	OL-SW	89
14	Bell Rib	170077	460c	-	426	-	OL-SW	89
15	Stirrup Crag	176092	616	113	225	-	OL-SW	89

I. SCOAT FELL

109

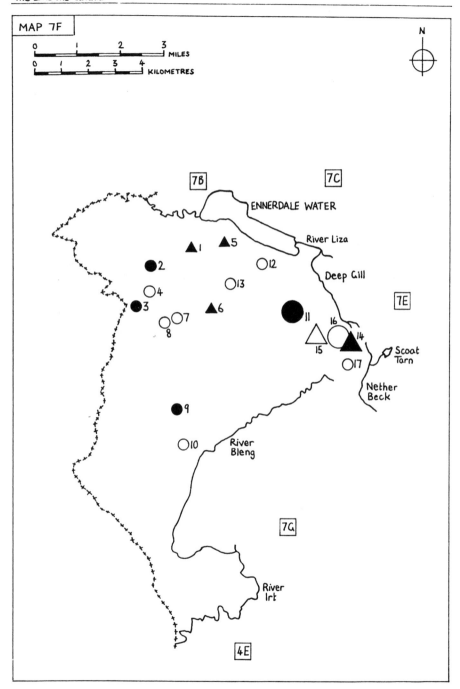

MAP 7F

0   1   2   3 MILES
0   1   2   3   4 KILOMETRES

N

7B   7C

ENNERDALE WATER

River Liza

▲1   ▲5

●2   ○12   Deep Gill

○4   ○13   7E

●3   ○7
    ○8   ▲6   ●11
                    16
              △   ○ ▲14
              15   Scoat
                        ○17   Tarn

●9   Nether
                          Beck

○10   River
      Bleng

7G

River
Irt

4E

TABLE 7F
THE WESTERN FELLS - ENNERDALE

| No. | Name | Grid ref. | Ht. | No. in order of altitude | | | OS map no. | |
				Fell	Top	AW	1:25000	1:50000
1	GRIKE	085141	488	170	393	177	OLNW	89
2	Blakeley Rise	070135	389	213	533	-	OLNW	89
3	Swarth Fell	065120	335	233	587	-	OL-NW	89
4	Burn Edge	069125	320c	-	609	-	OLNW	89
5	CRAG FELL	097144	523	153	334	162	OLNW	89
6	LANK RIGG	092120	541	138	306	152	OLNW	89
7	Kinniside Common	078116	375	-	544	-	OL-NW	89
8	Latter Barrow	074115	354	-	568	-	OLNW	89
9	Swainson Knott	079084	340c	230	579	-	OLSW	89
10	Ponsonby Fell	082071	310c	-	629	-	OLSW	89
11	Iron Crag [1]	123119	640c	103	193	-	OLNW	89
12	Boat How	111136	363	-	557	-	OLNW	89
13	Whoap	099129	511	-	354	-	OL-NW	89
14	HAYCOCK	145107	797	39	54	36	OLNW	89
15	CAW FELL	132110	690c	-	147	94	OLNW	89
16	Little Gowder Crag	140110	733x	-	108	-	OLNW	89
17	High Pikehow	144099	574	-	262	-	OLSW	89

1. Ennerdale Fell

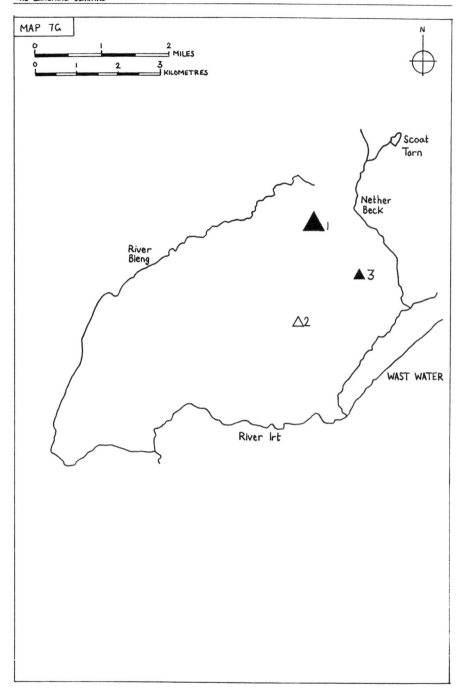

TABLE 7G
THE WESTERN FELLS - NETHER WASDALE

				No. in order of altitude			OS map no.	
No.	Name	Grid ref.	Ht.	Fell	Top	AW	1:25000	1:50000
1	SEATALLAN	140084	692	86	146	93	OL:SW	89
2	BUCKBARROW	136061	420c	-	475	197	OL:SW	89
3	MIDDLE FELL	151072	582	121	256	135	OL:SW	89

No. in order of altitude

Fell	Top	AW	Ht.	Name	Grid ref.	Ref.
1	1	1	978	SCAFELL PIKE	216072	4B-5
2	2	2	964	SCA FELL	207065	4B-12
-	3	-	950c	Symonds Knott	208068	4B-13
3	4	3	950	HELVELLYN	342151	1C-7
4	5	-	935	Ill Crag	223073	4B-9
5	6	4	931	SKIDDAW	260291	5E-6
6	7	-	930c	Broad Crag	219076	4B-7
-	8	-	925	Lower Man	337155	1C-8
7	9	5	910	GREAT END	227084	4B-10
8	10	6	902	BOW FELL	245064	4C-12
9	11	7	899	GREAT GABLE	211103	7D-12
10	12	8	892	PILLAR	171121	7E-7
-	13	9	891	NETHERMOST PIKE	344142	1C-13
11	14	10	890	CATSTYE CAM	348158	1C-6
12	15	11	885	ESK PIKE	237075	4C-4
13	16	12	883	RAISE	343174	1C-1
-	17	-	880c	High Crag	343137	1C-14
14	18	13	873	FAIRFIELD	359118	1D-2
15	19	14	868	BLENCATHRA	323277	5F-8
16	20	15	865	LITTLE MAN	267278	5E-12
17	21	16	863	WHITE SIDE	338167	1C-4
-	22	-	860c	Nameless summit (Bow Fell - N. Top)	245070	4C-13
-	23	-	860c	High Spying How	351149	1C-10
-	24	-	859x	Browncove Crags	332157	1C-9
18	25	17	859	CRINKLE CRAGS	249049	4C-17
19	26	18	858	DOLLYWAGGON PIKE	346131	1C-15
20	27	19	857	GREAT DODD	342206	1B-4
21	28	20	852	GRASMOOR	175203	6C-1
-	29	-	851	Gategill Fell	318274	5F-10
-	30	-	845	Foule Crag	324283	5F-9
22	31	21	843	STYBARROW DODD	343189	1B-13
23	32	22	841	LITTLE SCOAT FELL	160114	7E-1
24	33	23	841	ST SUNDAY CRAG	369134	1D-4
25	34	24	839	CRAG HILL	193204	6C-3
26	35	-	834x	Crinkle Crags	250046	4C-18
27	36	-	828	Black Crag	166117	7E-6
28	37	25	828	HIGH STREET	441111	2E-1
29	38	26	826	RED PIKE	165106	7E-11

No. in order of altitude

Fell	Top	AW	Ht.	Name	Grid ref.	Ref.
30	39	27	822	HART CRAG	368113	1D- 8
-	40	-	820c	Cofa Pike	359121	1D- 3
-	41	28	819	STEEPLE	157117	7E- 3
31	42	-	815	Shelter Crags	250053	4C-15
-	43	-	810	Pike de Bield	236068	4C- 6
32	44	29	807	HIGH STILE	170148	7C-10
-	45	-	804	Knowe Crags	312270	5F-11
33	46	30	803	THE OLD MAN OF CONISTON	272978	4F-18
-	47	-	802	Great Scoat Fell	155112	7E- 2
34	48	31	802	HIGH RAISE	448135	2B-12
35	49	32	802	KIRK FELL	195105	7D-13
36	50	33	802x	SWIRL HOW	273005	4F- 2
-	51	-	801	Black Crag	166101	7E-12
37	52	34	801	GREEN GABLE	215107	7D-11
38	53	35	800c	LINGMELL	209082	4B- 4
39	54	36	797	HAYCOCK	145107	7F-14
-	55	37	796	BRIM FELL	271986	4F-19
40	56	-	795	Green Side	353188	1B-14
41	57	38	792	DOVE CRAG	374105	1D-11
42	58	39	792	RAMPSGILL HEAD	443128	2B-22
43	59	40	791	GRISEDALE PIKE	198225	6B- 9
-	60	41	789	WATSON'S DODD	336196	1B-11
44	61	-	787	Nameless summit (Kirk Fell -E.Top)	199107	7D-14
45	62	42	785	ALLEN CRAGS	237085	4A- 9
-	63	-	784	Gavel Pike	373134	1D- 7
46	64	43	784	THORNTHWAITE CRAG	432101	2E- 4
47	65	44	783	GLARAMARA	245105	4A- 4
-	66	-	782	White Pike	169124	7E- 8
-	67	45	780c	GREAT CARRS	270009	4F- 3
-	68	46	780c	KIDSTY PIKE	447126	2B-24
-	69	-	780c	Pillar Rock	172124	7E-10
48	70	47	778	DOW CRAG	262978	4F-21
49	71	48	778	HARTER FELL	460093	2E-20
50	72	49	776	RED SCREES	396088	1E- 1
-	73	-	775	Looking Steads	246102	4A- 8
51	74	50	773	SAIL	198203	6C- 7
-	75	51	772	WANDOPE	188197	6G- 4
52	76	52	770c	GREY FRIAR	261005	4F- 1

No. in order of altitude

Fell	Top	AW	Ht.	Name	Grid ref.	Ref.
-	77	-	770c	Nameless summit (Shelter Crags - N. Top)	249057	4G-16
53	78	53	770	HOPEGILL HEAD	186222	6B- 5
-	79	-	768	Pen	221068	4B- 6
54	80	54	766	GREAT RIGG	356104	1D-17
55	81	55	763	STONY COVE PIKE	418100	2G- 1
56	82	56	762	HIGH RAISE	281095	3G-5
-	83	57	762x	SLIGHT SIDE	210050	4B-15
57	84	58	762	WETHERLAM	288011	4F-10
-	85	-	760c	Great How Crags	273999	4F- 5
-	86	59	760c	MARDALE ILL BELL	448101	2E-2
-	87	-	760c	Yeastyrigg Crags	237066	4G-7
58	88	60	757	ILL BELL	437077	2E-9
-	89	61	756	HART SIDE	359198	1B-15
-	90	-	756	Sand Hill	187219	6B- 7
59	91	62	755	RED PIKE	161154	7G-7
-	92	-	754	Low Raise	456138	2B-21
60	93	63	753	DALE HEAD	223153	6D-9
-	94	-	750c	Caudale Moor	413101	2G- 6
-	95	-	750c	Raven Crag	394084	1E-3
61	96	64	746	CARL SIDE	255281	5E-4
62	97	-	745x	Black Sails	283007	4F-7
-	98	-	744	Buck Pike	262972	4F-22
63	99	65	744	HIGH CRAG	180140	7G-11
-	100	-	741	Round How	220081	4B-11
-	101	-	740	Little Stand	250034	4G-19
64	102	-	739	Hobcarton Crag	194220	6B-12
-	103	66	739	THE KNOTT	437127	2B-23
65	104	67	737	ROBINSON	202169	6D-14
66	105	68	736	HARRISON STICKLE	282074	3D-5
67	106	69	736	SEAT SANDAL	344115	1D-1
68	107	70	734	LONG SIDE	249284	5E-1
-	108	-	733x	Little Gowder Crag	140110	7F-16
-	109	-	730c	Codale Head	289091	3G-7
-	110	-	730c	Combe Head	250109	4A-6
-	111	-	730c	Jenkin Hill	274275	5E-11
-	112	-	730c	Little How Crags	272997	4F-6
-	113	71	730c	SERGEANT MAN	286089	3G-6
69	114	72	730	KENTMERE PIKE	466078	2E-22

No in order of altitude

Fell	Top	AW	Ht.	Name	Grid ref.	Ref.
70	115	73	727	HINDSCARTH	216165	6D-11
71	116	74	726	CLOUGH HEAD	334225	1B-1
72	117	75	726	ULLSCARF	292122	3B-9
-	118	76	723	THUNACAR KNOTT	279080	3D-7
73	119	-	721	Nameless summit (Lincomb Tarns Top)	242097	4A-11
-	120	-	720c	Randerside	349211	1B-6
74	121	77	720	FROSWICK	435085	2E-8
75	122	-	719	Nameless summit (Gasgale Crags)	175221	6B-1
-	123	78	718	BIRKHOUSE MOOR	364160	1C-11
76	124	79	715	BRANDRETH	215119	7D-7
77	125	80	715	LONSCALE FELL	285271	5E-13
78	126	81	713	BRANSTREE	478100	2H-1
-	127	-	711	Red Crag	450152	2B-14
-	128	-	710c	Raven Howe	450145	2B-13
79	129	82	710	KNOTT	296330	5C-8
-	130	-	710	Nameless summit (Thornthwaite Crag- N. Ridge)	430110	2E-5
80	131	83	709	PIKE O'STICKLE	274073	3D-1
-	132	84	707	WHITESIDE	170219	6B-2
81	133	85	706	YOKE	438067	2E-10
82	134	86	705	PIKE OF BLISCO	271042	4D-1
-	135	-	703	Ladyside Pike	185227	6B-6
-	136	-	703	Nameless summit (Lonscale Fell - E. Top)	289273	5E-14
83	137	87	702	BOWSCALE FELL	333305	5F-1
84	138	88	701	COLD PIKE	263036	4C-24
-	139	-	700c	Middleboot Knotts	213081	4B-8
-	140	89	700c	PAVEY ARK	285079	3D-8
-	141	90	699	GRAY CRAG	428117	2E-6
-	142	91	697	GREY KNOTTS	217126	7D-8
-	143	-	696	Great Knott	260043	4C-20
85	144	92	696	REST DODD	432137	2A-14
-	145	-	692	Little Carrs	270014	4F-4
86	146	93	692	SEATALLAN	140084	7G-1
-	147	94	690c	CAW FELL	132110	7F-15
-	148	95	690c	ULLOCK PIKE	244288	5E-2
87	149	96	690	GREAT CALVA	291312	5C-16
-	150	-	684	Nameless summit (High House Tarn Top)	240092	4A-10
-	151	-	683	Cold Pike	259036	4C-25

No in order of altitude

Fell	Top	AW	Ht.	Name	Grid ref.	Ref.
88	152	97	683	BANNERDALE CRAGS	335290	5F-5
-	153	-	682	Brown Pike	261966	4F-23
-	154	-	682	Scales Fell	332279	5F-12
-	155	98	680c	LOFT CRAG	277071	3D-3
-	156	-	676	Cam Spout Crag	214055	4B-14
89	157	99	675	SHEFFIELD PIKE	369182	1B-22
-	158	100	673	BAKESTALL	266307	5E-8
-	159	-	673	Nameless summit (Branstree - E.Top)	488103	2H-2
90	160	101	672	SCAR CRAGS	208206	6C-11
91	161	102	671	LOADPOT HILL	457181	2B-1
-	162	-	670c	Nameless summit (Combe Door Top)	253109	4A-7
-	163	-	670c	Stang	354175	1C-2
-	164	103	670c	WETHER HILL	456167	2B-15
-	165	-	670c	Wether Hill	454163	2B-16
-	166	-	666	Adam Seat	471091	2E-21
-	167	-	666	Sale How	276286	5E-10
92	168	104	664	TARN CRAG	488078	2I-1
-	169	-	660c	Nameless summit (Bowscale Fell - E.Top)	341311	5F-2
-	170	-	660c	Calfhow Pike	331211	1B-5
93	171	105	660c	CARROCK FELL	342336	5D-8
-	172	-	660c	Nameless summit (Cold Pike - W.Top)	256037	4G-26
-	173	-	660c	High Kop	458160	2B-19
-	174	-	660c	Lingmell End	446092	2E-3
94	175	106	660	WHITELESS PIKE	180190	6C-5
95	176	107	658	HIGH PIKE	319350	5D-1
96	177	108	657	PLACE FELL	406170	2A-2
-	178	109	656	HIGH PIKE	374088	1D-13
-	179	-	656	Low Saddle	288133	3B-11
97	180	110	655	SELSIDE PIKE	490112	2H-3
-	181	111	654	MIDDLE DODD	397096	1E-2
98	182	112	653	HARTER FELL	219997	4H-1
99	183	113	653x	HIGH SPY	234162	6D-3
-	184	114	651	GREAT SCA FELL	291339	5C-11
-	185	-	650c	Long Crag	154122	7E-4
100	186	115	650c	ROSSETT PIKE	249075	4C-1
-	187	-	650c	Tongue Head	241080	4C-5
101	188	116	648	FLEETWITH PIKE	206142	7D-3
102	189	117	646	BASE BROWN	225115	7D-10

No in order of altitude

Fell	Top	AW	Ht.	Name	Grid ref.	Ref.
-	190	-	644	Snarker Pike	390075	IE-4
-	191	-	642	Little Calva	282315	5C-17
-	192	-	641	Dodd	164157	7C-9
103	193	-	640c	Iron Crag	123119	7F-11
-	194	-	640c	Rainsborrow Crag	441068	2E-11
-	195	-	640c	Thorn Crag	280071	3D-4
104	196	118	638	GREY CRAG	497072	21-2
105	197	119	637	CAUSEY PIKE	219209	6C-12
-	198	-	637	Harrop Pike	501078	21-3
106	199	120	637	LITTLE HART CRAG	387100	1D-15
-	200	-	634	Hobcarton End	195235	6B-10
-	201	121	633	MUNGRISDALE COMMON	312292	5F-13
107	202	122	633	STARLING DODD	142158	7C-5
108	203	-	632	Seathwaite Fell	227097	4B-1
-	204	-	631	Nameless summit (Seathwaite Fell - S.Top)	228094	4B-3
-	205	-	630c	Blea Crag	236171	6D-6
109	206	-	630c	Dovenest Crag	256114	4A-2
-	207	-	630c	Honister Crag	213141	7D-4
-	208	-	630c	Little Sca Fell	290342	5C-10
-	209	-	630c	Round How	408166	2A-5
110	210	-	628	Rough Crag	454112	2E-7
111	211	123	628	YEWBARROW	173085	7E-13
-	212	-	627x	Coomb Height	310327	5G-15
-	213	-	627	Hare Stones	316344	5D-4
-	214	-	627	Looking Stead	186118	7E-9
-	215	-	626	Goat Scar	473069	2E-23
-	216	124	622	BIRKS	380144	1D-5
-	217	-	621	Rydal Fell	357087	1D-18
-	218	-	621	Walna Scar	258963	4G-1
-	219	-	620c	Drygill Head	318342	5D-5
-	220	-	620c	Pike How	411090	2C-4
-	221	-	620c	White Pike	339229	1B-3
-	222	125	618	HARTSOP DODD	411118	2C-2
112	223	126	616	GREAT BORNE	124164	7C-1
-	224	-	616	Great Lingy Hill	310340	5D-6
113	225	-	616	Stirrup Crag	176092	7E-15
-	226	-	615x	Lad Stones	292998	4F-16

No in order of altitude

Fell	Top	AW	Ht	Name	Grid ref.	Ref.
-	227	127	612	HERON PIKE	356083	1D-19
-	228	-	612	Rosthwaite Cam	256118	4A-3
-	229	-	610c	Heron Pike	373178	1B-23
-	230	-	610c	Raven Crag	419111	2C-3
-	231	-	610c	Standing Crag	296134	3B-12
-	232	-	610	Brown Crag	328177	1C-5
-	233	-	610	Tewit How	145119	7E-5
114	234	128	609	ILLGILL HEAD	169049	4E-1
-	235	-	609	Iron Crag	304339	5D-7
115	236	129	608	HIGH SEAT	287180	3A-10
-	237	-	608	White Maiden	254957	4G-2
-	238	-	607	Miton Hill	329341	5D-10
-	239	-	606	Buck Pike	253078	4C-2
-	240	-	604	Nameless summit (Bowscale Fell-Far E.Top)	348311	5F-3
-	241	-	603	Round Knott	334337	5D-9
-	242	130	601	SEATHWAITE FELL	229102	4B-2
-	243	-	600c	Little Lingy Hill	302334	5C-14
116	244	-	600	Black Combe	135855	4I-18
-	245	-	598	White Pike	249956	4G-3
117	246	131	597	HAY STACKS	193131	7D-1
118	247	-	593	St Raven's Edge	406084	2C-7
-	248	-	590c	Great Yarlside	521079	2I-10
-	249	-	590c	Hart Crag	413086	2C-5
-	250	-	590c	Pike	303320	5C-13
119	251	132	590	BLEABERRY FELL	286196	3A-2
-	252	-	590	Little Dodd	149155	7C-8
120	253	-	588	Black Crags	255081	4C-3
-	254	133	587	SHIPMAN KNOTTS	473063	2E-24
-	255	134	586	BRAE FELL	289352	5C-9
121	256	135	582	MIDDLE FELL	151072	7G-3
122	257	136	581	ARD CRAGS	207198	6C-16
-	258	137	580c	HARTSOP ABOVE HOW	384120	1D-9
-	259	138	576	MAIDEN MOOR	237182	6D-4
123	260	139	576	THE NAB	434152	2A-18
-	261	-	575	High Brow	368214	1B-8
-	262	-	574	High Pikehow	144099	7F-17

No in order of altitude

Fell	Top	AW	Ht.	Name	Grid ref.	Ref.
-	263	-	574	Thornythwaite Fell	245119	4A-5
124	264	140	573	BLAKE FELL	110197	7B-2
125	265	-	573	Whitfell	159930	4I-11
-	266	-	572	Low Kop	474165	2B-20
126	267	141	571	SERGEANT'S CRAG	274114	3B-7
-	268	-	570c	Nameless summit (Bleaberry Fell- S.E.Top)	291191	3A-6
-	269	-	570c	Buck Crag	422139	2A-16
-	270	-	570c	High Gait Crags	230058	4C-8
-	271	-	570	Burnt Horse	288280	5E-15
127	272	142	568	OUTERSIDE	211215	6C-8
-	273	-	568	The Band	261061	4C-14
128	274	143	567	ANGLETARN PIKES	414148	2A-10
-	275	-	565	Angletarn Pikes	414147	2A-11
-	276	-	565	Wasdale Pike	536084	2I-7
-	277	-	562	Herdus	118163	7C-2
-	278	144	561	BROCK CRAGS	417137	2A-15
129	279	-	561	Seat	186134	7C-12
-	280	-	560c	Great Saddle Crag	526084	2I-9
-	281	-	560c	Satura Crag	424137	2A-17
130	282	-	558	Bell Crags	298143	3A-15
131	283	145	556	KNOTT RIGG	197189	6C-14
-	284	-	554	Great Round How	207128	7D-5
132	285	146	553	STEEL FELL	319111	3C-1
-	286	-	553	Swineside Knott	379197	1B-17
133	287	-	553	Swinklebank Crag	501049	2J-1
-	288	-	553	The Tongue	348302	5F-4
134	289	147	552	LORD'S SEAT	204266	6A-8
-	290	-	550c	Erin Crag	283997	4F-8
-	291	-	550c	Heck Crag	418149	2A-13
-	292	-	550c	High Scawdel	233149	6D-10
-	293	-	550c	The Knight	404176	2A-3
-	294	-	550	Brown Hills	378194	1B-16
-	295	-	550	Common Fell	382205	1B-19
-	296	148	550	MEAL FELL	283337	5C-12
-	297	149	550	TARN CRAG	303093	3C-8
135	298	-	549	Buck Barrow	152910	4I-14
136	299	150	549	HARD KNOTT	232024	4C-21

No in order of altitude

Fell	Top	AW	Ht.	Name	Grid ref.	Ref.
-	300	·	547	Martcrag Moor	268083	3D-2
-	301	-	546	Nameless summit (Knott Rigg - N.Top)	200192	6C-15
137	302	-	544	Carling Knott	117203	7B-9
-	303	-	543	Burn Moor	151924	4I-13
-	304	-	541	Nameless summit (Ancrow Brow - N.Top)	503059	2J-2
·	305	151	541x	BLEA RIGG	302078	3C-10
138	306	152	541	LANK RIGG	092120	7F-6
-	307	-	541	Nameless summit (Matterdale Common)	364222	1B-7
-	308	-	540c	Ancrow Brow	500055	2J-3
139	309	153	540c	BESSYBOOT	258125	4A-1
·	310	-	540c	Lining Crag	283112	3B-16
-	311	-	540c	Watermillock Common	379203	1B-18
-	312	-	538	Hare Crag	277299	5E-9
140	313	154	537x	CALF CRAG	301104	3C-2
141	314	155	537	GREAT MELL FELL	397254	1A-1
-	315	-	535	Kinmont Buck Barrow	147910	4I-15
142	316	156	535	WHIN RIGG	152034	4E-2
-	317	157	532x	ARTHUR'S PIKE	461207	2B-3
143	318	-	531	High Wether Howe	515109	2I-12
-	319	-	530c	Blake Rigg	285039	4D-4
144	320	-	530	White Howe	524042	2J-9
145	321	-	529	Caw	230945	4G-9
-	322	-	529	High Crags	217175	6D-12
-	323	-	529	Rowantreethwaite	487122	2H-4
146	324	-	528	Green Crag	203131	7D-2
-	325	-	528	The Forest	528036	2J-10
147	326	158	526	GAVEL FELL	117185	7B-11
148	327	159	526	GREAT COCKUP	273333	5C-6
149	328	-	526	High Snockrigg	187169	6D-16
·	329	-	525	Demming Crags	222002	4H-2
150	330	-	525	Ullister Hill	209260	6A-13
151	331	160	525	WHINLATTER	197249	6A-16
-	332	161	524x	BONSCALE PIKE	453200	2B-2
152	333	-	524	Lord's Seat	518066	2I-22
153	334	162	523	CRAG FELL	097144	7F-5
-	335	·	522	Border End	228019	4G-22
154	336	-	522	Great How	197040	4B-20
155	337	163	522	SOUTHER FELL	355291	5F-6

No in order of altitude

Fell	Top	AW	Ht.	Name	Grid ref.	Ref.
-	338	-	521	Low Scawdel	243161	6D-8
-	339	-	520c	Birk Fell	296017	4F-11
-	340	164	520c	EAGLE CRAG	276121	3B-8
-	341	-	520c	Scam Matthew	516105	2I-18
-	342	165	519	HIGH HARTSOP DODD	394108	1D-16
-	343	-	517	Brown How	191251	6A-17
-	344	-	516	Little Yarlside	532072	2I-11
156	345	166	516	SALLOWS	437040	2E-17
-	346	167	515	HIGH TOVE	289165	3A-11
-	347	-	515	Seat Robert	527114	2I-17
-	348	-	514	Threlkeld Knotts	330230	1B-2
-	349	-	512	Capplebarrow	508034	2J-4
-	350	-	512	Gale Crag	392124	1D-10
157	351	168	512	MELLBREAK	149186	7B-18
-	352	169	511	BROOM FELL	196270	6A-10
-	353	-	511	West Fell	332355	5D-3
-	354	-	511	Whoap	099129	7F-13
-	355	-	510c	Birk Fell	403183	2A-4
-	356	-	510c	Long Moss	289148	3A-17
-	357	-	510c	Nameless summit (Souther Fell-S.Top)	352287	5F-7
158	358	170	509	BEDA HEAD	428170	2A-8
159	359	171	509	HEN COMB	132181	7B-16
160	360	-	509	Lowthwaite Fell	278347	5C-4
-	361	-	509	Nameless summit (Mellbreak-N.Top)	143195	7B-19
-	362	172	508	LOW PIKE	374078	1D-14
-	363	-	508	Nab Crags	312125	3B-14
-	364	-	505	Cockup	259314	5E-7
161	365	173	505	LITTLE MELL FELL	423240	1A-3
-	366	-	503	Hare Shaw	498131	2H-5
162	367	174	502	DODD	244213	5E-5
-	368	-	502x	Ulthwaite Rigg	514093	2I-4
-	369	-	501	Birk Hill	308355	5D-2
163	370	-	501	High Dodd	415182	2A-6
-	371	-	500c	Fewling Stones	513118	2I-13
-	372	-	500c	Sleddale Pike	535094	2I-6
-	373	175	500c	STONE ARTHUR	348092	1D-21
-	374	-	500c	Stony Rigg	411151	2A-12
-	375	-	500	Raw Pike	308076	3C-14

No in order of altitude

Fell	Top	AW	Ht.	Name	Grid ref.	Ref.
•	376	-	499	Gale Fell	144168	7C-6
-	377	-	499x	Yew Bank	232031	4C-23
-	378	-	498	Stainton Pike	153943	4I-12
-	379	-	497	Low How	374215	1B-9
-	380	-	496x	Seat How	213256	6A-14
164	381	-	495	High House Bank	543048	2I-24
-	382	-	494	Little Round How	207132	7D-6
165	383	-	494	Yoadcastle	157952	4I-6
166	384	-	493	Bannisdale Fell	516052	2J-8
167	385	-	493	Robin Hood	530059	2I-23
-	386	-	493	Tarbarrel Moss	206253	6A-15
-	387	-	490c	Belles Knott	297086	3C-9
-	388	-	490c	Great Castle How	308078	3C-12
-	389	-	490	Castle Crag	446052	2E-12
168	390	-	489	Nameless summit (Bampton Common)	487165	2B-7
169	391	176	489	GREEN CRAG	200983	4H-9
-	392	-	488	Nameless summit (Gavel Fell - N.Top)	120189	7B-12
170	393	177	488	GRIKE	085141	7F-1
171	394	178	487	BAYSTONES	404053	2D-1
-	395	-	487	High Scarth Crag	215044	4B-16
172	396	-	485	Whatshaw Common	542061	2I-20
-	397	-	484	Wansfell Pike	394042	2D-2
-	398	-	484	Nameless summit (Whatshaw Common - E.Top)	548062	2I-21
-	399	-	484x	Middle Crag	288158	3A-14
173	400	179	483	LONGLANDS FELL	276354	5C-2
-	401	-	483	Middle How	296110	3B-15
174	402	180	483	SOUR HOWES	428032	2E-18
-	403	-	482	Sharp Knott	107201	7B-5
175	404	181	481	GOWBARROW FELL	408218	1A-9
-	405	-	480c	Little Castle How	310076	3C-13
-	406	-	480c	Woodend Height	157954	4I-7
-	407	182	479	ARMBOTH FELL	297160	3A-13
176	408	-	477	Hesk Fell	176947	4I-4
-	409	183	475	BURNBANK FELL	110209	7B-4
-	410	-	475	Force Crag	196213	6B-8
-	411	-	475	High Pen	110189	7B-6
-	412	-	472	Stoupdale Crags	151874	4I-19

No in order of altitude Fell	Top	AW	Ht.	Name	Grid ref.	Ref.
-	413	-	470c	Aikin Knott	215199	6C-17
-	414	-	470c	Gowk Hill	445167	2B-17
-	415	-	470c	Stangs	382113	1D-12
-	416	-	470c	Whitegill Crag	298072	3C-11
177	417	-	469	Crook Crag	200987	4H-7
178	418	184	469	LINGMOOR FELL	303046	4D-5
179	419	-	469	Pikes	238947	4G-8
-	420	185	468x	BARF	214268	6A-12
-	421	-	465	Powley's Hill	505135	2H-6
-	422	-	464	Gowbarrow Park	408214	1A-10
-	423	-	463	Brown Rigg	305146	3A-16
180	424	186	461	RAVEN CRAG	305188	3A-8
-	425	-	461x	Seatoller Fell	233132	7D-9
-	426	-	460c	Bell Rib	170077	7E-14
-	427	-	460c	Dodd Crag	291206	3A-5
181	428	-	456	Nameless summit (Banna Fell - E. Top)	116174	7B-13
182	429	187	456	GRAYSTONES	178264	6A-5
183	430	188	455	BARROW	227218	6C-10
184	431	-	455	Cockley Moor	381225	1B-12
-	432	-	454	Dodd	169231	6B-3
185	433	-	452	Long Fell	557085	2I-19
186	434	189	451	CAT BELLS	244199	6D-1
-	435	-	451	Dod Hill	411053	2D-3
-	436	-	451	Floutern Cop	122174	7B-15
-	437	-	450c	High Crag	274139	3B-10
-	438	-	448	Plough Fell	162912	4I-16
187	439	190	447	BINSEY	225355	5A-1
188	440	-	447	Knock Murton	095191	7B-10
189	441	-	447	Stile End	221219	6C-9
190	442	-	446	Sippling Crag	302193	3A-7
-	443	-	445	Capple Howe	432029	2E-19
-	444	-	444	Brownthwaite Crag	443174	2B-18
-	445	-	444	White How	205975	4H-10
191	446	191	442	GLENRIDDING DODD	381175	1B-24
-	447	-	442	White Pike	151956	4I-9
192	448	192	440c	GREAT CRAG	270147	3B-6
-	449	-	440c	Great Ladstones	532122	2I-16
-	450	193	440c	NAB SCAR	355072	1D-20

No in order of altitude

Fell	Top	AW	Ht.	Name	Grid ref.	Ref.
-	451	-	440c	Tongue Rigg	530100	2I-5
-	452	-	439	Scar Lathing	226049	4C-9
-	453	-	438	Kirk Fell	173266	6A-7
193	454	-	437	Great Meldrum	415223	1A-6
-	455	-	435	Kit Crag	492143	2H-7
-	456	-	435	Kitty Crag	295990	4F-14
-	457	194	433	ARNISON CRAG	394150	1D-6
-	458	-	433	Horsehow Crags	224008	4H-3
-	459	-	433	Rowling End	229207	6C-13
194	460	195	432	STEEL KNOTTS	440181	2B-11
-	461	-	430c	High Snab Bank	213179	6D-15
-	462	-	430c	Wallow Crag	496149	2H-8
-	463	-	429	Sleddale Forest	488016	2F-6
-	464	-	428	Hawk Rigg	300017	4F-12
195	465	-	427	Brunt Knott	484006	2F-5
196	466	-	427	Great Worm Crag	194969	4H-13
-	467	-	427	Hazel Bank	545077	2I-8
197	468	-	426	Hollow Moor	469040	2F-1
-	469	-	426	Lad Hows	172193	6C-2
-	470	-	426	Low Forest	502150	2H-9
198	471	-	424	Nameless summit (Little Mell Fell - S.Top)	425233	1A-4
-	472	-	423	Blake Rigg	301012	4F-13
199	473	196	423	LOW FELL	137226	7A-6
-	474	-	422x	Stoneside Hill	146893	4I-17
-	475	197	420c	BUCKBARROW	136061	7G-2
-	476	-	420c	Fisher Crag	305163	3A-12
-	477	198	420c	GIBSON KNOTT	319099	3C-3
-	478	-	420c	Pianet Knott	234046	4G-10
-	479	-	420c	Rowantree Knotts	450052	2E-14
-	480	-	420c	White Knott	469215	2B-4
-	481	-	419	Harper Hills	508143	2H-12
200	482	199	416	FELLBARROW	132242	7A-1
-	483	-	415	Four Stones Hill	492163	2B-8
-	484	-	414	Lang How	318071	3C-16
-	485	-	413	Whin Ben	166213	6B-4
-	486	-	412	High Crags	237190	6D-5
-	487	-	412	Nameless summit (Low Fell)	136223	7A-7
-	488	-	411	Banna Fell	109175	7B-14

No in order of altitude Fell	Top	AW	Ht.	Name	Grid ref	Ref
-	489	-	410c	Broughton Moor	251943	4G-5
201	490	200	410c	BRUND FELL	264162	3B-4
202	491	-	410c	Ether Knott	268172	3B-1
-	492	-	410c	Nameless summit (Hollow Moor - E.Top)	473042	2F-2
-	493	-	410c	Hugh's Laithes Pike	502152	2H-10
-	494	-	410c	Kennel Crag	285990	4F-9
-	495	-	410c	Nitting Haws	243168	6D-7
-	496	-	410c	Scope End	224183	6D-13
203	497	-	410c	Sourfoot Fell	135233	7A-5
-	498	-	410c	Swinescar Pike	313072	3C-15
-	499	-	409	Owsen Fell	101209	7B-3
-	500	-	408	Iron Crag	211972	4H-11
204	501	-	408x	Low Fell	303022	4F-17
-	502	-	407	Piked Howes	450048	2E-13
-	503	-	406x	Knotts	482204	2B-5
205	504	201	405	HELM CRAG	327093	3G-4
-	505	-	405	Langhowe Pike	530131	2I-14
-	506	-	404	Dow Crag	204995	4H-8
-	507	-	404	Little Meldrum	422228	1A-5
-	508	-	404	Nameless summit (Peathill Crag- S.Top)	227012	4H-4
206	509	-	404	Throstlehow Crag	227043	4C-11
-	510	-	404	Widow Hause	183269	6A-9
-	511	-	401	Todd Fell	512021	2J-5
-	512	-	400c	Castle Crag	300188	3A-9
207	513	-	400c	Knotts	261144	3B-5
-	514	-	400c	Little Birkhouse Hill	494165	2B-9
-	515	-	400c	Peathill Crag	228013	4H-5
-	516	-	400c	Rowantree Crag	529128	2I-15
-	517	-	400c	Rowantree How	157959	4I-8
-	518	-	397	Dawsonground Crags	204027	4B-22
208	519	-	397	Whiteside Pike	521015	2J-6
-	520	-	396	Gray Stones	161873	4I-21
-	521	-	395	Nameless summit (Brunt Knott-S.Top)	489998	2F-7
-	522	-	395	Irton Fell	144026	4E-3
-	523	-	395	Nameless summit (Naddle Farm Top)	505152	2H-11
209	524	202	395	SILVER HOW	325066	3C-17
-	525	-	395	Silverybield Crag	212039	4B-17
210	526	-	392	King's How	258166	3B-3

No in order of altitude

Fell	Top	AW	Ht.	Name	Grid ref.	Ref.
211	527	-	391	Darling Fell	128225	7A-8
-	528	-	390c	Brown Howe	266047	4D-2
-	529	-	390c	Kettle Crag	279048	4D-3
-	530	-	390c	Pike How	288069	3D-6
-	531	-	390c	Smithy Fell	133237	7A-4
212	532	-	390	Nameless summit (Potter Fell)	497003	2F-8
213	533	-	389	Blakeley Rise	070135	7F-2
214	534	203	388	HALLIN FELL	433198	2A-1
-	535	-	387	Round How	392208	1B-20
215	536	-	385	Fox Haw	223936	4G-11
-	537	-	385	Hatteringill Head	134248	7A-2
-	538	-	380c	Pinnacle Howe	497167	2B-10
-	539	-	380	Swindale Foot Crag	518139	2H-14
-	540	204	379	WALLA CRAG	277213	3A-3
-	541	-	378	Sleet Fell	422188	2A-7
-	542	-	376	Raven Crag	166883	4I-20
216	543	-	375x	Heughscar Hill	488231	2B-6
-	544	-	375	Kinniside Common	078116	7F-7
217	545	-	375	Stickle Pike	212927	4G-14
-	546	-	374	Kinn	219232	6B-11
218	547	205	373	LING FELL	180286	6A-4
-	548	-	370c	Bracken How	393211	1B-21
-	549	-	370c	Wallowbarrow Heald	215973	4H-12
219	550	-	370	The Pike	186934	4I-5
-	551	-	369	Cat Crag	209031	4B-21
220	552	206	368	LATRIGG	279247	5E-16
-	553	-	367	Lamb Pasture	534021	2J-11
-	554	-	365	Cocklaw Fell	481038	2F-3
-	555	-	365	Godworth	101183	7B-7
221	556	207	364	THE TONGUE	422064	2E-16
-	557	-	363	Boat How	111136	7F-12
-	558	-	361	Nameless summit (Raven's Crag)	224929	4G-12
-	559	-	360c	Brown Dodd	266177	3B-2
-	560	-	360c	Little Dodd	132192	7B-17
-	561	-	360c	Scale Knotts	455056	2E-15
-	562	-	360c	Side Pike	293053	4D-6
-	563	-	359x	Pike	286218	3A-4
222	564	208	359	SALE FELL	194297	6A-1

No in order of altitude

Fell	Top	AW	Ht.	Name	Grid ref.	Ref.
-	565	-	357x	Birk Crag	315135	3B-13
223	566	209	355	RANNERDALE KNOTTS	167182	6C-6
-	567	-	354	High Pike Haw	264949	4G-4
-	568	-	354	Latter Barrow	074115	7F-8
-	569	-	350c	Heron Crag	220033	4B-18
224	570	-	345	Eycott Hill	386295	5B-2
-	571	-	345	Lowthwaite	203297	6A-3
225	572	-	343	Brock Barrow	220943	4G-10
226	573	-	343	Fauids Brow	299307	5G-18
227	574	210	343	HIGH RIGG	307215	3A-1
-	575	-	342	Brock Crag	215029	4B-19
228	576	-	342	Hagg Wood	428220	1A-7
229	577	-	342	Knipe Scar	527191	2G-1
-	578	-	342	In Scar	536191	2G-2
230	579	-	340c	Swainson Knott	079084	7F-9
-	580	-	339	Castle Rock	322197	1B-10
-	581	-	338	Scale Knott	149178	7B-20
-	582	-	338x	Scalebarrow Knott	520153	2H-13
-	583	-	338	Skelgill Bank	245206	6D-2
231	584	-	337	Boat How	177034	4E-5
232	585	211	335	LOUGHRIGG FELL	347051	3C-18
-	586	-	335	Rivings	198294	6A-2
233	587	-	335	Swarth Fell	065120	7F-3
234	588	-	335	The Bell	288979	4F-20
235	589	-	335	Top O' Selside	309919	4J-3
236	590	-	333	Bowness Knott	112155	7C-4
-	591	-	333	Watches	241304	5E-3
-	592	-	332	Nameless summit (Lamb Pasture - S.E.Top)	539018	2J-12
-	593	-	332x	The Knott	243932	4G-6
-	594	-	332x	Ulgraves	511996	2F-9
-	595	-	331	The Knott	144951	4I-10
-	596	-	331	Wolf Howe	543024	2J-13
237	597	-	330c	Great How	313187	1C-3
-	598	-	330c	Little Eycott Hill	385301	5B-3
-	599	-	330c	The Swirls	319163	1C-12
-	600	-	330c	Winter Crag	430183	2A-9
-	601	-	329	Great Bank	144019	4E-4

No in order of altitude

Fell	Top	AW	Ht.	Name	Grid ref.	Ref.
238	602	–	328	Kepple Crag	199 999	4H-6
239	603	212	323	BLACK CRAG	340 016	4D-7
240	604	–	322	Arnsbarrow Hill	311 911	4J-5
241	605	–	322×	Latrigg	246 355	5A-2
242	606	–	321×	Green How	258 375	5C-1
243	607	–	321	Gummer's How	390 885	2K-1
–	608	–	320c	Brown How	116 158	7C-3
–	609	–	320c	Burn Edge	069 125	7F-4
–	610	–	320c	Heel Toe Hill	313 919	4J-4
–	611	–	320c	Yewdale Crag	308 993	4F-15
–	612	–	319×	Birk Crag	430 218	1A-8
–	613	–	319	Embleton High Common	167 274	6A-6
244	614	–	319	Rough Crag	161 978	4I-2
–	615	–	318	Birch Fell	395 892	2K-2
–	616	–	318	Burthwaite Heights	189 283	6A-11
245	617	213	317	HOLME FELL	315 006	4D-8
–	618	–	316	Nameless summit (Arnsbarrow Hill - S.Top)	310 908	4J-6
–	619	–	316	Mickle Rigg	273 369	5C-3
246	620	–	314	Carron Crag	325 943	4J-1
247	621	–	313	High Hows	096 202	7B-1
248	622	–	312	Goat Crag	204 018	4B-24
–	623	–	312	Lofshaw Hill	387 278	5B-5
249	624	–	311	Keldas	385 163	1C-16
–	625	–	311	Kelton Fell	095 181	7B-8
–	626	–	311	Nameless summit (Lowthwaite Fell-W.Top)	267 353	5C-5
250	627	–	311	Seat How	165 971	4I-3
–	628	–	311	White Hall Knott	156 855	4I-22
–	629	–	310c	Ponsonby Fell	082 071	7F-10
–	630	–	310c	Tarn Hill	209 923	4G-16
251	631	–	308	Hutton Roof	373 341	5B-1
–	632	–	307	Nameless summit (Park Head Road Top)	218 935	4G-13
–	633	–	306	Nameless summit (Whin Fell)	135 255	7A-3
–	634	–	305	Brownhow Hill	408 266	1A-2
–	635	–	305	Castle How	257 342	5C-7
–	636	–	305	Great Stickle	212 916	4G-15
252	637	–	305	Water Crag	154 975	4I-1

No in order of altitude

Fell	Top	AW	Ht.	Name		Grid ref	Ref
253	638	-	303	Banks		269940	4G-7
-	639	-	303		Greenah Crag	396284	5B-4
254	640	-	302	Dacre Bank		451276	1A-11
255	641	-	302	Park Crags		311935	4J-2
-	642	-	300c		Bull How	206020	4B-25
-	643	-	300c		Murthwaite Knott	518009	2J-7
-	644	-	300c		Peelplace Noddle	196022	4B-23
256	645	-	300	Millrigg Knott		464011	2F-4
257	646	214	290	CASTLE CRAG		250160	6D-17

Name Ht. Grid ref.	Type	Date	Notes
☐ Adam Seat 666 471091	◯		
☐ Aikin Knott 470c 215199	○		
☐ ALLEN CRAGS 785 237085	▲		
☐ Ancrow Brow 540c 500055	○		
☐ Ancrow Brow - N.Top 541 503059	○		
☐ ANGLETARN PIKES 567 414148	▲		
☐ Angletarn Pikes 565 414147	○		
☐ ARD CRAGS 581 207198	▲		
☐ ARMBOTH FELL 479 297160	△		
☐ ARNISON CRAG 433 394150	△		
☐ Arnsbarrow Hill 322 311911	●		
☐ Arnsbarrow Hill - S.Top 316 310908	○		
☐ ARTHUR'S PIKE 532x 461207	△		
☐ BAKESTALL 673 266307	△		
☐ Bampton Common 489 487165	●		
☐ Banks 303 269940	●		
☐ Banna Fell 411 109175	○		
☐ Banna Fell - E.Top 456 116174	●		
☐ BANNERDALE CRAGS 683 335290	▲		

Name						
Ht.	Grid ref.		Type	Date	Notes	
☐ Bannisdale Fell			●			
493	516052					
☐ BARF			△			
468x	214268					
☐ BARROW			▲			
455	227218					
☐ BASE BROWN			▲			
646	225115					
☐ BAYSTONES			▲			
487	404053					
☐ BEDA HEAD			▲			
509	428170					
☐ Bell Crags			●			
558	298143					
☐ Bell Rib			○			
460c	170077					
☐ Belles Knott			○			
490c	297086					
☐ BESSYBOOT			▲			
540c	258125					
☐ BINSEY			▲			
447	225355					
☐ Birch Fell			○			
318	395892					
☐ Birk Crag			○			
357x	315135					
☐ Birk Crag			○			
319x	430218					
☐ Birk Fell			○			
520c	296017					
☐ Birk Fell			○			
510c	403183					
☐ Birk Hill			○			
501	308355					
☐ BIRKHOUSE MOOR			△			
718	364160					
☐ BIRKS			△			
622	380144					

133

Name		Date	Notes
Ht.	Grid ref.	Type	

☐ Black Combe
  600   135855 ●

☐ BLACK CRAG
  323   340016 ▲

☐ Black Crag
  828   166117 ●

☐ Black Crag
  801   166101 ○

☐ Black Crags
  588   255081 ●

☐ Black Sails
  745x 283007 ●

☐ BLAKE FELL
  573   110197 ▲

☐ Blake Rigg
  530c 285039 ○

☐ Blake Rigg
  423   301012 ○

☐ Blakeley Rise
  389   070135 ●

☐ Blea Crag
  630c 236171 ○

☐ BLEA RIGG
  541x 302078 △

☐ BLEABERRY FELL
  590   286196 ▲

☐ Bleaberry Fell - S.E. Top
  570c 291191 ○

☐ BLENCATHRA
  868   323277 ▲

☐ Boat How
  363   111136 ○

☐ Boat How
  337   177034 ●

☐ BONSCALE PIKE
  524x 453200 △

☐ Border End
  522   228019 ○

Name Ht. Grid ref.	Type	Date	Notes
☐ BOW FELL 902 245064	▲	— —	— —
☐ Bow Fell - N.Top 860c 245070	◯	— —	— —
☐ Bowness Knott 333 112 155	●	— —	— —
☐ BOWSCALE FELL 702 333305	▲	— —	— —
☐ Bowscale Fell - E.Top 660c 341 311	◯	— —	— —
☐ Bowscale Fell - Far E.Top 604 348 311	◯	— —	— —
☐ Bracken How 370c 393 211	◯	— —	— —
☐ BRAE FELL 586 289352	△	— —	— —
☐ BRANDRETH 715 215119	▲	— —	— —
☐ BRANSTREE 713 478100	▲	— —	— —
☐ Branstree - E.Top 673 488103	◯	— —	— —
☐ BRIM FELL 796 271986	△	— —	— —
☐ Broad Crag 930c 219076	●	— —	— —
☐ Brock Barrow 343 220943	●	— —	— —
☐ Brock Crag 342 215029	◯	— —	— —
☐ BROCK CRAGS 561 417137	△	— —	— —
☐ BROOM FELL 511 196270	△	— —	— —
☐ Broughton Moor 410c 251943	◯	— —	— —
☐ Brown Crag 610 328177	◯	— —	— —

135

Name		Type	Date	Notes
Ht.	Grid ref.			

☐ Brown Dodd
  360c 266177 ○ ———— ————

☐ Brown Hills
  550 378194 ○ ———— ————

☐ Brown How
  517 191251 ○ ———— ————

☐ Brown How
  320c 116158 ○ ———— ————

☐ Brown Howe
  390c 266047 ○ ———— ————

☐ Brown Pike
  682 261966 ○ ———— ————

☐ Brown Rigg
  463 305146 ○ ———— ————

☐ Browncove Crags
  859x 332157 ○ ———— ————

☐ Brownhow Hill
  305 408266 ○ ———— ————

☐ Brownthwaite Crag
  444 443174 ○ ———— ————

☐ BRUND FELL
  410c 264162 ▲ ———— ————

☐ Brunt Knott
  427 484006 ● ———— ————

☐ Brunt Knott - S.Top
  395 489998 ○ ———— ————

☐ Buck Barrow
  549 152910 ● ———— ————

☐ Buck Crag
  570c 422139 ○ ———— ————

☐ Buck Pike
  744 262972 ○ ———— ————

☐ Buck Pike
  606 253078 ○ ———— ————

☐ BUCKBARROW
  420c 136061 △ ———— ————

☐ Bull How
  300c 206020 ○ ———— ————

Name		Date	Notes
Ht.	Grid ref.	Type	

- ☐ Burn Edge — 320c 069125 — ○
- ☐ Burn Moor — 543 151924 — ○
- ☐ BURNBANK FELL — 475 110209 — △
- ☐ Burnt Horse — 570 288280 — ○
- ☐ Burthwaite Heights — 318 189283 — ○
- ☐ CALF CRAG — 537x 301104 — ▲
- ☐ Calfhow Pike — 660c 331211 — ○
- ☐ Cam Spout Crag — 676 214055 — ○
- ☐ Capple Howe — 445 432029 — ○
- ☐ Capplebarrow — 512 508034 — ○
- ☐ CARL SIDE — 746 255281 — ▲
- ☐ Carling Knott — 544 117203 — ●
- ☐ CARROCK FELL — 660c 342336 — ▲
- ☐ Carron Crag — 314 325943 — ●
- ☐ Castle Crag — 490 446052 — ○
- ☐ Castle Crag — 400c 300188 — ○
- ☐ CASTLE CRAG — 290 250160 — ▲
- ☐ Castle How — 305 257342 — ○
- ☐ Castle Rock — 339 322197 — ○

Name		Type	Date	Notes
Ht.	Grid ref.			
☐ CAT BELLS		▲		
451	244199			
☐ Cat Crag		○		
369	209031			
☐ CATSTYE CAM		▲		
890	348158			
☐ Caudale Moor		○		
750c	413101			
☐ CAUSEY PIKE		▲		
637	219209			
☐ Caw		●		
529	230945			
☐ CAW FELL		△		
690c	132110			
☐ CLOUGH HEAD		▲		
726	334225			
☐ Cocklaw Fell		○		
365	481038			
☐ Cockley Moor		●		
455	381225			
☐ Cockup		○		
505	259314			
☐ Codale Head		○		
730c	289091			
☐ Cofa Pike		○		
820c	359121			
☐ COLD PIKE		▲		
701	263036			
☐ Cold Pike		○		
683	259036			
☐ Cold Pike - W. Top		○		
660c	256037			
☐ Combe Door Top		○		
670c	253109			
☐ Combe Head		○		
730c	250109			
☐ Common Fell		○		
550	382205			

Name	Date	Notes
Ht. Grid ref.	Type	

☐ Coomb Height
627x   310327   ○ ————   ————————

☐ CRAG FELL
523   097144   ▲ ————   ————————

☐ CRAG HILL
839   193204   ▲ ————   ————————

☐ CRINKLE CRAGS
859   249049   ▲ ————   ————————

☐ Crinkle Crags
834x   250046   ● ————   ————————

☐ Crook Crag
469   200987   ● ————   ————————

☐ Dacre Bank
302   451276   ● ————   ————————

☐ DALE HEAD
753   223153   ▲ ————   ————————

☐ Darling Fell
391   128225   ● ————   ————————

☐ Dawsonground Crags
397   204027   ○ ————   ————————

☐ Demming Crags
525   222002   ○ ————   ————————

☐ Dod Hill
451   411053   ○ ————   ————————

☐ Dodd
641   164157   ○ ————   ————————

☐ DODD
502   244273   ▲ ————   ————————

☐ Dodd
454   169231   ◑ ————   ————————

☐ Dodd Crag
460c   291206   ○ ————   ————————

☐ DOLLYWAGGON PIKE
858   346131   ▲ ————   ————————

☐ DOVE CRAG
792   374105   ▲ ————   ————————

☐ Dovenest Crag
630c   256114   ● ————   ————————

Name Ht. Grid ref.	Type	Date	Notes
☐ DOW CRAG 778 262978	▲		
☐ Dow Crag 404 204995	○		
☐ Drygill Head 620c 318342	◯		
☐ EAGLE CRAG 520c 276121	△		
☐ Embleton High Common 319 167274	○		
☐ Erin Crag 550c 283997	○		
☐ ESK PIKE 885 237075	▲		
☐ Ether Knott 410c 268172	●		
☐ Eycott Hill 345 386295	●		
☐ FAIRFIELD 873 359118	▲		
☐ Faulds Brow 343 299307	●		
☐ FELLBARROW 416 132242	▲		
☐ Fewling Stones 500c 513118	○		
☐ Fisher Crag 420c 305163	○		
☐ FLEETWITH PIKE 648 206142	▲		
☐ Floutern Cop 451 122174	○		
☐ Force Crag 475 196213	○		
☐ Foule Crag 845 324283	◯		
☐ Four Stones Hill 415 492163	○		

Name		Date	Notes
Ht. Grid ref.	Type		

- [ ] Fox Haw
  385 223936 ● ___ ___
- [ ] FROSWICK
  720 435085 ▲ ___ ___
- [ ] Gale Crag
  512 392124 ○ ___ ___
- [ ] Gale Fell
  499 144168 ○ ___ ___
- [ ] Gasgale Crags
  719 175221 ● ___ ___
- [ ] Gategill Fell
  851 318274 ◯ ___ ___
- [ ] GAVEL FELL
  526 117185 ▲ ___ ___
- [ ] Gavel Fell - N.Top
  488 120189 ○ ___ ___
- [ ] Gavel Pike
  784 373134 ◯ ___ ___
- [ ] GIBSON KNOTT
  420c 319099 △ ___ ___
- [ ] GLARAMARA
  783 245105 ▲ ___ ___
- [ ] GLENRIDDING DODD
  442 381175 ▲ ___ ___
- [ ] Goat Crag
  312 204018 ● ___ ___
- [ ] Goat Scar
  626 473069 ◯ ___ ___
- [ ] Godworth
  365 101183 ○ ___ ___
- [ ] GOWBARROW FELL
  481 408218 ▲ ___ ___
- [ ] Gowbarrow Park
  464 408214 ○ ___ ___
- [ ] Gowk Hill
  470c 445167 ○ ___ ___
- [ ] GRASMOOR
  852 175203 ▲ ___ ___

Name			Date	Notes
Ht.	Grid ref.	Type		

☐ GRAY CRAG
699   428117   △ ————— ——————————

☐ Gray Stones
396   161873   ○ ————— ——————————

☐ GRAYSTONES
456   178264   ▲ ————— ——————————

☐ Great Bank
329   144019   ○ ————— ——————————

☐ GREAT BORNE
616   124164   ▲ ————— ——————————

☐ GREAT CALVA
690   291312   ▲ ————— ——————————

☐ GREAT CARRS
780c   270009   △ ————— ——————————

☐ Great Castle How
490c   308078   ○ ————— ——————————

☐ GREAT COCKUP
526   273333   ▲ ————— ——————————

☐ GREAT CRAG
440c   270147   ▲ ————— ——————————

☐ GREAT DODD
857   342206   ▲ ————— ——————————

☐ GREAT END
910   227084   ▲ ————— ——————————

☐ GREAT GABLE
899   211103   ▲ ————— ——————————

☐ Great How
522   197040   ● ————— ——————————

☐ Great How
330c   313187   ● ————— ——————————

☐ Great How Crags
760c   273999   ◯ ————— ——————————

☐ Great Knott
696   260043   ◯ ————— ——————————

☐ Great Ladstones
440c   532122   ○ ————— ——————————

☐ Great Lingy Hill
616   310340   ◯ ————— ——————————

Name		Date	Notes
Ht.	Grid ref.	Type	

☐ Great Meldrum
437   415223   ●

☐ GREAT MELL FELL
537   397254   ▲

☐ GREAT RIGG
766   356104   ▲

☐ Great Round How
554   207128   ○

☐ Great Saddle Crag
560c   526084   ○

☐ GREAT SCA FELL
651   291339   △

☐ Great Scoat Fell
802   155112   ○

☐ Great Stickle
305   212916   ○

☐ Great Worm Crag
427   194969   ●

☐ Great Yarlside
590c   521079   ○

☐ Green Crag
528   203131   ●

☐ GREEN CRAG
489   200983   ▲

☐ GREEN GABLE
801   215107   ▲

☐ Green How
321x   258375   ●

☐ Green Side
795   353188   ●

☐ Greenah Crag
303   396284   ○

☐ GREY CRAG
638   497072   ▲

☐ GREY FRIAR
770c   261005   ▲

☐ GREY KNOTTS
697   217126   △

143

Name		Date	Notes
Ht.	Grid ref.	Type	

☐ **GRIKE**
488   085141   ▲

☐ **GRISEDALE PIKE**
791   198225   ▲

☐ Gummer's How
321   390885   ●

☐ Hagg Wood
342   428220   ●

☐ **HALLIN FELL**
388   433198   ▲

☐ **HARD KNOTT**
549   232024   ▲

☐ Hare Crag
538   277299   ○

☐ Hare Shaw
503   498131   ○

☐ Hare Stones
627   316344   ○

☐ Harper Hills
419   508143   ○

☐ **HARRISON STICKLE**
736   282074   ▲

☐ Harrop Pike
637   501078   ○

☐ **HART CRAG**
822   368113   ▲

☐ Hart Crag
590c   413086   ○

☐ **HART SIDE**
756   359198   △

☐ **HARTER FELL**
778   460093   ▲

☐ **HARTER FELL**
653   219997   ▲

☐ HARTSOP ABOVE HOW
580c   384120   △

☐ HARTSOP DODD
618   411118   △

Name / Ht. Grid ref.	Type	Date	Notes
☐ Hatteringill Head 385　134248	◯		
☐ Hawk Rigg 428　300017	◯		
☐ HAY STACKS 597　193131	▲		
☐ HAYCOCK 797　145107	▲		
☐ Hazel Bank 427　545077	◯		
☐ Heck Crag 550c　418149	◯		
☐ Heel Toe Hill 320c　313919	◯		
☐ HELM CRAG 405　327093	▲		
☐ HELVELLYN 950　342151	▲		
☐ HEN COMB 509　132181	▲		
☐ Herdus 562　118163	◯		
☐ Heron Crag 350c　220033	◯		
☐ HERON PIKE 612　356083	△		
☐ Heron Pike 610c　373178	◯		
☐ Hesk Fell 477　176947	●		
☐ Heughscar Hill 375x　488231	●		
☐ High Brow 575　368214	◯		
☐ High Crag 880c　343137	◯		
☐ HIGH CRAG 744　180140	▲		

Name		Type	Date	Notes
Ht.	Grid ref.			

☐ High Crag
450c 274139 ○ —————— ————————

☐ High Crags
529 217175 ○ —————— ————————

☐ High Crags
412 237190 ○ —————— ————————

☐ High Dodd
501 415182 ● —————— ————————

☐ High Gait Crags
570c 230058 ○ —————— ————————

☐ HIGH HARTSOP DODD
519 394108 △ —————— ————————

☐ High House Bank
495 543048 ● —————— ————————

☐ High House Tarn Top
684 240092 ◯ —————— ————————

☐ High Hows
313 096202 ● —————— ————————

☐ High Kop
660c 458160 ◯ —————— ————————

☐ High Pen
475 110189 ○ —————— ————————

☐ HIGH PIKE
658 319350 ▲ —————— ————————

☐ HIGH PIKE
656 374088 △ —————— ————————

☐ High Pike Haw
354 264949 ○ —————— ————————

☐ High Pikehow
574 144099 ○ —————— ————————

☐ HIGH RAISE
802 448135 ▲ —————— ————————

☐ HIGH RAISE
762 281095 ▲ —————— ————————

☐ HIGH RIGG
343 307215 ▲ —————— ————————

☐ High Scarth Crag
487 215044 ○ —————— ————————

Name		Date	Notes
Ht.	Grid ref.	Type	

☐ High Scawdel
550c   233149   ○ ————————   ————————

☐ HIGH SEAT
608   287180   ▲ ————————   ————————

☐ High Snab Bank
430c   213179   ○ ————————   ————————

☐ High Snockrigg
526   187169   ● ————————   ————————

☐ HIGH SPY
653x   234162   ▲ ————————   ————————

☐ High Spying How
860c   351149   ◯ ————————   ————————

☐ HIGH STILE
807   170148   ▲ ————————   ————————

☐ HIGH STREET
828   441111   ▲ ————————   ————————

☐ HIGH TOVE
515   289165   △ ————————   ————————

☐ High Wether Howe
531   515109   ● ————————   ————————

☐ HINDSCARTH
727   216165   ▲ ————————   ————————

☐ Hobcarton Crag
739   194220   ⬤ ————————   ————————

☐ Hobcarton End
634   195235   ◯ ————————   ————————

☐ Hollow Moor
426   469040   ● ————————   ————————

☐ Hollow Moor - E.Top
410c   473042   ○ ————————   ————————

☐ HOLME FELL
317   315006   ▲ ————————   ————————

☐ Honister Crag
630c   213141   ◯ ————————   ————————

☐ HOPEGILL HEAD
770   186222   ▲ ————————   ————————

☐ Horsehow Crags
433   224008   ○ ————————   ————————

Name			Date	Notes
Ht.	Grid ref.	Type		

☐ Hugh's Laithes Pike
410c   502152   ○

☐ Hutton Roof
308   373341   ●

☐ ILL BELL
757   437077   ▲

☐ Ill Crag
935   223073   ●

☐ ILLGILL HEAD
609   169049   ▲

☐ In Scar
342   536191   ○

☐ Iron Crag
640c   123119   ●

☐ Iron Crag
609   304339   ○

☐ Iron Crag
408   211972   ○

☐ Irton Fell
395   144026   ○

☐ Jenkin Hill
730c   274275   ○

☐ Keldas
311   385163   ●

☐ Kelton Fell
311   095181   ○

☐ Kennel Crag
410c   285990   ○

☐ KENTMERE PIKE
730   466078   ▲

☐ Kepple Crag
328   199999   ●

☐ Kettle Crag
390c   279048   ○

☐ KIDSTY PIKE
780c   447126   △

☐ King's How
392   258166   ●

Name		Date	Notes
Ht. Grid ref.	Type		
☐ Kinmont Buck Barrow	○		
535 147910			
☐ Kinn	○		
374 219232			
☐ Kinniside Common	○		
375 078116			
☐ KIRK FELL	▲		
802 195105			
☐ Kirk Fell - E.Top	●		
787 199107			
☐ Kirk Fell	○		
438 173266			
☐ Kit Crag	○		
435 492143			
☐ Kitty Crag	○		
435 295990			
☐ Knipe Scar	●		
342 527191			
☐ Knock Murton	●		
447 095191			
☐ KNOTT	▲		
710 296330			
☐ KNOTT RIGG	▲		
556 197189			
☐ Knott Rigg - N.Top	○		
546 200192			
☐ Knotts	○		
406x 482204			
☐ Knotts	●		
400c 267144			
☐ Knowe Crags	◯		
804 312270			
☐ Lad Hows	○		
426 172193			
☐ Lad Stones	◯		
615x 292998			
☐ Ladyside Pike	◯		
703 185227			

Name		Type	Date	Notes
Ht.	Grid ref.			
☐ Lamb Pasture		○		
367	534021			
☐ Lamb Pasture - S.E.Top		○		
332	539018			
☐ Lang How		○		
414	318071			
☐ Langhowe Pike		○		
405	530131			
☐ LANK RIGG		▲		
541	092120			
☐ LATRIGG		▲		
368	279247			
☐ Latrigg		●		
322x	246355			
☐ Latter Barrow		○		
354	074115			
☐ Lincomb Tarns Top		●		
721	242097			
☐ LING FELL		▲		
373	180286			
☐ LINGMELL		▲		
800c	209082			
☐ Lingmell End		○		
660c	446092			
☐ LINGMOOR FELL		▲		
469	303046			
☐ Lining Crag		○		
540c	283112			
☐ Little Birkhouse Hill		○		
400c	494165			
☐ Little Calva		○		
642	282315			
☐ Little Carrs		○		
692	270014			
☐ Little Castle How		○		
480c	310076			
☐ Little Dodd		○		
590	149155			

Name	Date	Notes
Ht. Grid ref.	Type	

☐ Little Dodd
360c 132192 ○

☐ Little Eycott Hill
330c 385301 ○

☐ Little Gowder Crag
733x 140110 ○

☐ LITTLE HART CRAG
637 387100 ▲

☐ Little How Crags
730c 272997 ○

☐ Little Lingy Hill
600c 302334 ○

☐ LITTLE MAN
865 267278 ▲

☐ Little Meldrum
404 422228 ○

☐ LITTLE MELL FELL
505 423240 ▲

☐ Little Mell Fell - S.Top
424 425233 ●

☐ Little Round How
494 207132 ○

☐ Little Sca Fell
630c 290342 ○

☐ LITTLE SCOAT FELL
841 160114 ▲

☐ Little Stand
740 250034 ○

☐ Little Yarlside
516 532072 ○

☐ LOADPOT HILL
671 457181 ▲

☐ Lofshaw Hill
312 387278 ○

☐ LOFT CRAG
680c 277071 △

☐ Long Crag
650c 154122 ○

Name Ht. Grid ref.	Type	Date	Notes
☐ Long Fell 452 557085	●		
☐ Long Moss 510c 289148	○		
☐ LONG SIDE 734 249284	▲		
☐ LONGLANDS FELL 483 276354	▲		
☐ LONSCALE FELL 715 285271	▲		
☐ Lonscale Fell - E.Top 703 289273	◯		
☐ Looking Stead 627 186118	◯		
☐ Looking Steads 775 246102	◯		
☐ LORD'S SEAT 552 204266	▲		
☐ Lord's Seat 524 518066	●		
☐ LOUGHRIGG FELL 335 347051	▲		
☐ LOW FELL 423 137226	▲		
☐ Low Fell 408x 303022	●		
☐ Low Fell 412 136223	○		
☐ Low Forest 426 502150	○		
☐ Low How 497 374215	○		
☐ Low Kop 572 474165	○		
☐ LOW PIKE 508 374078	△		
☐ Low Raise 754 456138	◯		

Name			Date	Notes
Ht.	Grid ref.	Type		
☐ Low Saddle		◯		
656	288133			
☐ Low Scawdel		○		
521	243161			
☐ Lower Man		◯		
925	337155			
☐ Lowthwaite		○		
345	203297			
☐ Lowthwaite Fell		●		
509	278347			
☐ Lowthwaite Fell -W.Top		○		
311	267353			
☐ MAIDEN MOOR		△		
576	237182			
☐ MARDALE ILL BELL		△		
760c	448101			
☐ Martcrag Moor		○		
547	268083			
☐ Matterdale Common		○		
541	364222			
☐ MEAL FELL		△		
550	283337			
☐ MELLBREAK		▲		
512	149186			
☐ Mellbreak - N.Top		○		
509	143195			
☐ Mickle Rigg		○		
316	273369			
☐ Middle Crag		○		
484x	288158			
☐ MIDDLE DODD		△		
654	397096			
☐ MIDDLE FELL		▲		
582	151072			
☐ Middle How		○		
483	296110			
☐ Middleboot Knotts		◯		
700c	213081			

Name Ht. Grid ref.	Type	Date	Notes
Millrigg Knott 300 464011	●		
Miton Hill 607 329341	○		
MUNGRISDALE COMMON 633 312292	△		
Murthwaite Knott 300c 518009	○		
Nab Crags 508 312125	○		
NAB SCAR 440c 355072	△		
Naddle Farm Top 395 505152	○		
NETHERMOST PIKE 891 344142	△		
Nitting Haws 410c 243168	○		
OUTERSIDE 568 211215	▲		
Owsen Fell 409 101209	○		
Park Crags 302 311935	●		
Park Head Road Top 307 218935	○		
PAVEY ARK 700c 285079	△		
Peathill Crag 400c 228013	○		
Peathill Crag - S.Top 404 227012	○		
Peelplace Noddle 300c 196022	○		
Pen 768 221068	○		
Pianet Knott 420c 234046	○		

Name / Ht.	Grid ref.	Type	Date	Notes
☐ Pike 590c	303320	○		
☐ Pike 359x	286218	○		
☐ Pike de Bield 810	236068	◯		
☐ Pike How 620c	411090	◯		
☐ Pike How 390c	288069	○		
☐ PIKE O'STICKLE 709	274073	▲		
☐ PIKE OF BLISCO 705	271042	▲		
☐ Piked Howes 407	450048	○		
☐ Pikes 469	238947	●		
☐ PILLAR 892	171121	▲		
☐ Pillar Rock 780c	172124	◯		
☐ Pinnacle Howe 380c	497167	○		
☐ PLACE FELL 657	406170	▲		
☐ Plough Fell 448	162912	○		
☐ Ponsonby Fell 310c	082071	○		
☐ Potter Fell 390	497003	●		
☐ Powley's Hill 465	505135	○		
☐ Rainsborrow Crag 640c	441068	◯		
☐ RAISE 883	343174	▲		

Name		Type	Date	Notes
Ht.	Grid ref			
☐ RAMPSGILL HEAD		▲		
792	443128			
☐ Randerside		◯		
720c	349211			
☐ RANNERDALE KNOTTS		▲		
355	167182			
☐ Raven Crag		◯		
750c	394084			
☐ Raven Crag		◯		
610c	419111			
☐ RAVEN CRAG		▲		
461	305188			
☐ Raven Crag		◯		
376	166883			
☐ Raven Howe		◯		
710c	450145			
☐ Raven's Crag		◯		
361	224929			
☐ Raw Pike		◯		
500	308076			
☐ Red Crag		◯		
711	450152			
☐ RED PIKE		▲		
826	165106			
☐ RED PIKE		▲		
755	161154			
☐ RED SCREES		▲		
776	396088			
☐ REST DODD		▲		
696	432137			
☐ Rivings		◯		
335	198294			
☐ Robin Hood		●		
493	530059			
☐ ROBINSON		▲		
737	202169			
☐ ROSSETT PIKE		▲		
650c	249075			

Name		Date	Notes
Ht.	Grid ref.	Type	

☐ Rosthwaite Cam
  612   256 118

☐ Rough Crag
  628   454 112

☐ Rough Crag
  319   161 978

☐ Round How
  741   220 081

☐ Round How
  630c 408 166

☐ Round How
  387   392 208

☐ Round Knott
  603   334 337

☐ Rowantree Crag
  400c 529 128

☐ Rowantree How
  400c 157 959

☐ Rowantree Knotts
  420c 450 052

☐ Rowantreethwaite
  529   487 122

☐ Rowling End
  433   229 207

☐ Rydal Fell
  621   357 087

☐ SAIL
  773   198 203

☐ SALE FELL
  359   194 297

☐ Sale How
  666   276 286

☐ SALLOWS
  516   437 040

☐ Sand Hill
  756   187 219

☐ Satura Crag
  560c 424 137

Name			Date	Notes
Ht.	Grid ref.	Type		

☐ SCA FELL
964 207065 ▲

☐ SCAFELL PIKE
978 216072 ▲

☐ Scale Knott
338 149178 ○

☐ Scale Knotts
360c 455056 ○

☐ Scalebarrow Knott
338x 520153 ○

☐ Scales Fell
682 332279 ◯

☐ Scam Matthew
520c 516105 ○

☐ SCAR CRAGS
672 208206 ▲

☐ Scar Lathing
439 226049 ○

☐ Scope End
410c 224183 ○

☐ Seat
561 186134 ●

☐ Seat How
496x 213256 ○

☐ Seat How
311 165971 ●

☐ Seat Robert
515 527114 ○

☐ SEAT SANDAL
736 344115 ▲

☐ SEATALLAN
692 140084 ▲

☐ Seathwaite Fell
632 227097 ●

☐ SEATHWAITE FELL
601 229102 △

☐ Seathwaite Fell - S.Top
631 228094 ◯

Name Ht. Grid ref.	Type	Date	Notes
☐ Seatoller Fell 461x 233132	○		
☐ SELSIDE PIKE 655 490112	▲		
☐ SERGEANT MAN 730c 286089	△		
☐ SERGEANT'S CRAG 571 274114	▲		
☐ Sharp Knott 482 107201	○		
☐ SHEFFIELD PIKE 675 369182	▲		
☐ Shelter Crags 815 250053	●		
☐ Shelter Crags - N.Top 770c 249057	◯		
☐ SHIPMAN KNOTTS 587 473063	△		
☐ Side Pike 360c 293053	○		
☐ SILVER HOW 395 325066	▲		
☐ Silverybield Crag 395 222039	○		
☐ Sippling Crag 446 302193	●		
☐ Skelgill Bank 338 245206	○		
☐ SKIDDAW 931 260291	▲		
☐ Sleddale Forest 429 488016	○		
☐ Sleddale Pike 500c 535094	○		
☐ Sleet Fell 378 422188	○		
☐ SLIGHT SIDE 762x 210050	△		

Name		Type	Date	Notes
Ht. Grid ref.				
☐ Smithy Fell	○			
390c 133237				
☐ Snarker Pike	○			
644 390075				
☐ SOUR HOWES	▲			
483 428032				
☐ Sourfoot Fell	●			
410c 135233				
☐ SOUTHER FELL	▲			
522 355291				
☐ Souther Fell - S.Top	○			
510c 352287				
☐ St Raven's Edge	●			
593 406084				
☐ ST SUNDAY CRAG	▲			
841 369134				
☐ Stainton Pike	○			
498 153943				
☐ Standing Crag	○			
610c 296134				
☐ Stang	○			
670c 354175				
☐ Stangs	○			
470c 382113				
☐ STARLING DODD	▲			
633 142158				
☐ STEEL FELL	▲			
553 319 111				
☐ STEEL KNOTTS	▲			
432 440181				
☐ STEEPLE	△			
819 157117				
☐ Stickle Pike	●			
375 212927				
☐ Stile End	●			
447 221219				
☐ Stirrup Crag	●			
616 176092				

Name		Type	Date	Notes
Ht.	Grid ref			
☐ STONE ARTHUR		△		
500c	348092			
☐ Stoneside Hill		○		
422x	146893			
☐ STONY COVE PIKE		▲		
763	418100			
☐ Stony Rigg		○		
500c	411151			
☐ Stoupdale Crags		○		
472	151874			
☐ STYBARROW DODD		▲		
843	343189			
☐ Swainson Knott		●		
340c	079084			
☐ Swarth Fell		●		
335	065120			
☐ Swindale Foot Crag		○		
380	518139			
☐ Swinescar Pike		○		
410c	313072			
☐ Swineside Knott		○		
553	379197			
☐ Swinklebank Crag		●		
553	501049			
☐ SWIRL HOW		▲		
802x	273005			
☐ Symonds Knott		○		
950c	208068			
☐ Tarbarrel Moss		○		
493	206253			
☐ TARN CRAG		▲		
664	488078			
☐ TARN CRAG		△		
550	303093			
☐ Tarn Hill		○		
310c	209923			
☐ Tewit How		○		
610	145119			

	Name			Date	Notes
	Ht.	Grid ref.	Type		

☐ The Band
568   261061   ○

☐ The Bell
335   288979   ●

☐ The Forest
528   528036   ○

☐ The Knight
550c   404176   ○

☐ THE KNOTT
739   437127   △

☐ The Knott
332x   243932   ○

☐ The Knott
331   144951   ○

☐ THE NAB
576   434152   ▲

☐ THE OLD MAN OF CONISTON
803   272978   ▲

☐ The Pike
370   186934   ●

☐ The Swirls
330c   319163   ○

☐ The Tongue
553   348302   ○

☐ THE TONGUE
364   422064   ▲

☐ Thorn Crag
640c   280071   ○

☐ THORNTHWAITE CRAG
784   432101   ▲

☐ Thornthwaite Crag - N.Ridge
710   430110   ○

☐ Thornythwaite Fell
574   245119   ○

☐ Threlkeld Knotts
514   330230   ○

☐ Throstlehow Crag
404   227043   ●

Name	Type	Date	Notes
Ht. Grid ref.			
☐ THUNACAR KNOTT	△		
723 279080			
☐ Todd Fell	○		
401 512021			
☐ Tongue Head	◯		
650c 241080			
☐ Tongue Rigg	○		
440c 530100			
☐ Top O'Selside	●		
335 309919			
☐ Ulgraves	○		
332x 511996			
☐ Ullister Hill	●		
525 209260			
☐ ULLOCK PIKE	△		
690c 244288			
☐ ULLSCARF	▲		
726 292122			
☐ Ulthwaite Rigg	○		
502x 514093			
☐ WALLA CRAG	△		
379 277213			
☐ Wallow Crag	○		
430c 496149			
☐ Wallowbarrow Heald	○		
370c 215973			
☐ Walna Scar	◯		
621 258963			
☐ WANDOPE	△		
772 188197			
☐ Wansfell Pike	○		
484 394042			
☐ Wasdale Pike	○		
565 536084			
☐ Watches	○		
333 241304			
☐ Water Crag	●		
305 154975			

Name Ht. Grid ref.	Type	Date	Notes
☐ Watermillock Common 540c 379203	○		
☐ WATSON'S DODD 789 336196	△		
☐ West Fell 511 332355	○		
☐ WETHER HILL 670c 456167	△		
☐ Wether Hill 670c 454163	◯		
☐ WETHERLAM 762 288011	▲		
☐ Whatshaw Common 485 542061	●		
☐ Whatshaw Common - E.Top 484 548062	○		
☐ Whin Ben 413 166213	○		
☐ Whin Fell 306 135255	○		
☐ WHIN RIGG 535 152034	▲		
☐ WHINLATTER 525 197249	▲		
☐ White Hall Knott 311 156855	○		
☐ White How 444 205915	○		
☐ White Howe 530 524042	●		
☐ White Knott 420c 469215	○		
☐ White Maiden 608 254957	◯		
☐ White Pike 782 169124	◯		
☐ White Pike 620c 339229	◯		

Name		Date	Notes
Ht.	Grid ref.	Type	

- [ ] White Pike
  598   249956   ○
- [ ] White Pike
  442   151956   ○
- [ ] WHITE SIDE
  863   338167   ▲
- [ ] Whitegill Crag
  470c   298072   ○
- [ ] WHITELESS PIKE
  660   180190   ▲
- [ ] WHITESIDE
  707   170219   △
- [ ] Whiteside Pike
  397   521015   ●
- [ ] Whitfell
  573   159930   ●
- [ ] Whoap
  511   099129   ○
- [ ] Widow Hause
  404   183269   ○
- [ ] Winter Crag
  330c   430183   ○
- [ ] Wolf Howe
  331   543024   ○
- [ ] Woodend Height
  480c   157954   ○
- [ ] Yeastyrigg Crags
  760c   237066   ◯
- [ ] Yew Bank
  499x   232031   ○
- [ ] YEWBARROW
  628   173085   ▲
- [ ] Yewdale Crag
  320c   308993   ○
- [ ] Yoadcastle
  494   157952   ●
- [ ] YOKE
  706   438067   ▲

Adam Seat	2E-21	Birk Hill	5D-2
Aikin Knott	6C-17	BIRKHOUSE MOOR	IC-II
ALLEN CRAGS	4A-9	BIRKS	ID-5
Ancrow Brow	2J-3	Black Combe	4I-18
Ancrow Brow - N.Top[NS]	2J-2	BLACK CRAG	4D-7
ANGLETARN PIKES	2A-10	Black Crag	7E-6
Angletarn Pikes	2A-11	Black Crag	7E-12
ARD CRAGS	6C-16	Black Crags	4C-3
ARMBOTH FELL	3A-13	Black Fell - see BLACK CRAG	
ARNISON CRAG	ID-6	Black Sails	4F-7
Arnsbarrow Hill	4J-5	Black Star - see Honister Crag	
Arnsbarrow Hill - S.Top[NS]	4J-6	BLAKE FELL	7B-2
ARTHUR'S PIKE	2B-3	Blake Rigg	4D-4
Artlecrag Pike - see BRANSTREE		Blake Rigg	4F-13
Atkinson Pike - see Foule Crag		Blakeley Rise	7F-2
Aughertree Fell - see Green How		Blea Crag	6D-6
		Blea Crags - see High Snab Bank	
BAKESTALL	5E-8	BLEA RIGG	3C-10
Bampton Common[NS]	2B-7	BLEABERRY FELL	3A-2
Banks	4C-7	Bleaberry Fell - S.E.Top[NS]	3A-6
Banna Fell	7B-14	Bleaberry Knott - see Birk Fell	
Banna Fell - E.Top[NS]	7B-13	Blease Fell - see Knowe Crags	
BANNERDALE CRAGS	5F-5	BLENCATHRA	5F-8
Bannisdale Fell	2J-8	Boat How	4E-5
BARF	6A-12	Boat How	7F-12
BARROW	6C-10	BONSCALE PIKE	2B-2
BASE BROWN	7D-10	Border End	4C-22
BAYSTONES	2D-1	BOW FELL	4C-12
BEDA FELL - see BEDA HEAD		Bow Fell - N.Top[NS]	4C-13
BEDA HEAD	2A-8	BOWFELL- see BOW FELL	
Bell Crags	3A-15	Bowness Knott	7C-4
Bell Rib	7E-14	BOWSCALE FELL	5F-1
Belles Knott	3C-9	Bowscale Fell - E.Top[NS]	5F-2
BESSYBOOT	4A-1	Bowscale Fell - Far E.Top[NS]	5F-3
BINSEY	5A-1	Bracken How	IB-21
Birch Fell	2K-2	BRAE FELL	5C-9
Birk Crag	IA-8	BRANDRETH	7D-7
Birk Crag	3B-13	BRANSTREE	2H-1
Birk Fell	2A-4	Branstree - E.Top[NS]	2H-2
Birk Fell	4F-11	BRIM FELL	4F-19

HIGH RAISE	3C-5	Kennel Crag	4F-9
HIGH RIGG	3A-1	KENTMERE PIKE	2E-22
High Scarth Crag	4B-16	Kepple Crag	4H-6
High Scawdel	6D-10	Kettle Crag	4D-3
HIGH SEAT	3A-10	KIDSTY PIKE	2B-24
High Snab Bank	6D-15	King's How	3B-3
High Snockrigg	6D-16	Kinmont Buck Barrow	4I-15
HIGH SPY	6D-3	Kinn	6B-11
High Spying How	1C-10	Kinniside Common	7F-7
HIGH STILE	7C-10	Kirk Fell	6A-7
HIGH STREET	2E-1	KIRK FELL	7D-13
HIGH TOVE	3A-11	Kirk Fell - E.Top [NS]	7D-14
High Wether Howe	2I-12	Kit Crag	2H-7
High White Stones - see HIGH RAISE		Kitty Crag	4F-14
HINDSCARTH	6D-11	Knipe Scar	2G-1
Hobcarton Crag	6B-12	Knock Murton	7B-10
Hobcarton End	6B-10	KNOTT	5C-8
Hollow Moor	2F-1	KNOTT RIGG	6C-14
Hollow Moor -E.Top [NS]	2F-2	Knott Rigg - N.Top [NS]	6C-15
HOLME FELL	4D-8	Knotts	2B-5
Honister Crag	7D-4	Knotts	3B-5
HOPEGILL HEAD	6B-5	Knowe Crags	5F-11
Horsehow Crags	4H-3		
Hugh's Laithes Pike	2H-10	Lad Hows	6C-2
Hutton Roof	5B-1	Lad Stones	4F-16
		Ladyside Pike	6B-6
ILL BELL	2E-9	Lamb Pasture	2J-11
Ill Crag	4B-9	Lamb Pasture - S.E.Top [NS]	2J-12
ILLGILL HEAD	4E-1	Lang How	3C-16
In Scar	2G-2	Langhowe Pike	2I-14
Iron Crag	4H-11	LANK RIGG	7F-6
Iron Crag	5D-7	Latrigg	5A-2
Iron Crag	7F-11	LATRIGG	5E-16
Irton Fell	4E-3	Latter Barrow	7F-8
		Lincomb Tarns Top [NS]	4A-11
Jenkin Hill	5E-11	LING FELL	6A-4
John Bell's Banner -see STONY COVE PIKE		LINGMELL	4B-4
		Lingmell End	2E-3
Keldas	1C-16	LINGMOOR FELL	4D-5
Kelton Fell	7B-8	Lining Crag	3B-16

The summits

Over 600m	Separate fell	'Wainwright'	Symbol
✓	✓	✓	▲
✓	✓	✗	●
✓	✗	✓	△
✓	✗	✗	○
✗	✓	✓	▲
✗	✓	✗	●
✗	✗	✓	△
✗	✗	✗	○

This extract is taken from the full key on page 13.

We publish guides to individual towns, plus books on walking and cycling in the great outdoors throughout England and Wales. This is a recent selection:

The Lake District

FULL DAYS ON THE FELLS – Adrian Dixon (£7.95)
100 LAKE DISTRICT HILL WALKS – Gordon Brown (£7.95)
LAKELAND ROCKY RAMBLES: Geology beneath your feet – Brian Lynas (£7.95)
PUB WALKS IN THE LAKE DISTRICT – Neil Coates (£6.95)
LAKELAND WALKING, ON THE LEVEL – Norman Buckley (£6.95)
MOSTLY DOWNHILL: LEISURELY WALKS, LAKE DISTRICT – Alan Pears (£6.95)
THE THIRLMERE WAY – Tim Cappelli (£6.95)
THE FURNESS TRAIL – Tim Cappelli (£6.95)
CYCLING IN THE LAKE DISTRICT – John Wood (£7.95)

Other destinations . . .

LOG BOOK OF THE MOUNTAINS OF ENGLAND – Mark Woosey (£9.95)
LOG BOOK OF THE MOUNTAINS OF WALES – Mark Woosey (£7.95)
FIFTY CLASSIC WALKS IN THE PENNINES – Terry Marsh (£8.95)
EAST CHESHIRE WALKS – Graham Beech (£5.95)
RAMBLES AROUND MANCHESTER – Mike Cresswell (£5.95)
YORKSHIRE DALES WALKING: On The Level – Norman Buckley (£6.95)
WALKS IN MYSTERIOUS WALES – Laurence Main (£7.95)
CHALLENGING WALKS: NW England & N Wales – Ron Astley (£7.95)
BEST PUB WALKS – CHESTER & THE DEE VALLEY – John Haywood (£6.95)
BEST PUB WALKS IN GWENT – Les Lumsdon (£6.95)
BEST PUB WALKS IN POWYS – Les Lumsdon & Chris Rushton (£6.95)
BEST PUB WALKS IN PEMBROKESHIRE – Laurence Main (£6.95)
BEST PUB WALKS IN THE NORTH PENNINES – Nick Channer (£6.95)

There are many more titles in our fabulous series of 'Best Pub Walks' books for just about every popular walking area in the UK, all featuring access by public transport. All of our books are available from your local bookshop. In case of difficulty, or to obtain our complete catalogue, please contact:

SIGMA LEISURE, 1 SOUTH OAK LANE, WILMSLOW, CHESHIRE SK9 6AR
Phone: 01625 – 531035   Fax: 01625 – 536800

ACCESS and VISA orders welcome – call our friendly sales staff or use our 24 hour Answerphone service! Most orders are despatched on the day we receive your order – you could be enjoying our books in just a couple of days. Please add £2 p&p to all orders.